The Development of Deep Learning Technologies

Center for Electronics and Information Studies,
Chinese Academy of Engineering

The Development of Deep Learning Technologies

Research on the Development of Electronic
Information Engineering Technology
in China

Center for Electronics and Information Studies
Chinese Academy of Engineering
Beijing, China

ISBN 978-981-15-4583-2   ISBN 978-981-15-4584-9   (eBook)
https://doi.org/10.1007/978-981-15-4584-9

This Springer imprint is published by the registered company Springer Nature Singapore Pte Ltd.
The registered company address is: 152 Beach Road, #21-01/04 Gateway East, Singapore 189721, Singapore

Preface

The Research on the Development of Electronic Information Engineering Technology in China Book Series

In today's world, the wave of information technologies featured by digitalization, networking, and intelligence is gaining momentum. Information technologies are experiencing rapid changes with each passing day and are fully applied in production and life, bringing about profound changes in global economic, political, and security landscapes. Among diverse information technologies, electronic information engineering technology is one of the most innovative and widely used technologies and plays its greatest role in driving the development of other S&T fields. It is not only a field of intense competition in technological innovation, but also an important strategic direction for key players to fuel economic growth and seek competitive advantages over other players. Electronic information engineering technology is a typical "enabling technology" that enables technological progress in almost all other fields. Its integration with biotechnology, new energy technology, and new material technology is expected to set off a new round of technological revolution and industrial transformation, thereby bringing about new opportunities for the evolution of human society. Electronic information is a typical "engineering technology" and one of the most straightforward and practical tools. It realizes direct and close integration of scientific discoveries and technological innovations with industrial developments, greatly speeding up technological progress. Hence, it is regarded as a powerful force to change the world. Electronic information engineering technology is a vital driving force of China's rapid economic and social development in the past seven decades, especially in the past four decades of reform and opening up. Looking ahead, advances and innovations in electronic information engineering technology will remain to be one of the most important engines driving human progress.

CAE is China's foremost academic and advisory institution in engineering and technological sciences. Guided by the general development trends of science and technology around the world, CAE is committed to providing scientific, forward-looking, and timely advice for innovation-driven scientific and technological progress from a strategic and long-term perspective. CAE's mission is to function as a national high-end think tank. To fulfill the mission, the Division of Information and Electronic Engineering, under the guidance of its Vice President Zuoning Chen, Director Xicheng Lu, and the Standing Committee, mobilized more than 300 academicians and experts to jointly compile the General Section and the Special Themes of this book (hereinafter referred to as the "Blue Book"). The first stage of compilation was headed by Academicians Jiangxing Wu and Manqing Wu (from the end of 2015 to June 2018), and the second one was headed by Academicians Shaohua Yu and Jun Lu (since September 2018). The purposes of compiling the Blue Book are:

By analyzing technological progress and introducing major breakthroughs and marked achievements made in the electronic information field both at home and abroad each year to provide reference for China's scientific and technical personnel to accurately grasp the development trend of the field and provide support for China's policymakers to formulate related development strategies.

The "Blue Book" is compiled according to the following principles:

1. **Ensure appropriate description of annual increment**. The field of electronic information engineering technology enjoys a broad coverage and high development speed. Thus, the General Section should ensure an appropriate description of the annual increment, which is about the recent progress, new characteristics, and new trends.

2. **Selection of hot points and highlight points**. China's technological development is still at a mixed stage where it needs to assume the role of follower, contender, and leader simultaneously. Hence, the Special Themes should seek to depict the developmental characteristics the industry it focuses on and should center on the "hot points" and "highlight points" along the development journey.

3. **Integration of General Section and Special Themes.** The program consists of two sections: the General Section and the Special Themes. The former adopts a macro perspective to discuss the global and Chinese development of electronic information engineering technology, and its outlook; the latter provides detailed descriptions of hot points and highlight points in the 13 subfields.

Application System
8. Underwater acoustic engineering
13. Computer application

Acquiring Perception

3. Sensing

5. Electromagnetic space

Computation and Control

10. Control
11. Cognition
12. Computer systems and software

Cyber Security

6. Network and communication

7. Cybersecurity

Common Basis
1. Microelectronics and Optoelectronics 2. Optical engineering
4. Measurement, metrology and Instruments
9. Electromagnetic field and electromagnetic environment effect

Classification Diagrams of 13 Subfields of information and electronic engineering technology

The above graphic displays 5 categories and 13 subcategories, or special themes that bear distinct granularity. However, every subfield is closely connected with each other in terms of technological correlations, which allows easier matching with their corresponding disciplines.

Currently, the compilation of the "Blue Book" is still at a trial stage where careless omissions are unavoidable. Hence, we welcome comments and corrections.

The Development of Deep Learning Technologies in Research on the Development of Electronic Information Engineering Technology in China Book Series

Artificial Intelligence (AI), the primary driver of the new round of the science and technology revolution and industrial evolution, is affecting the world economy, society, and politics in a significant and unprecedented way. As a core AI breakthrough in the recent decade, deep learning has made enormous strides in both technology and application and has captured worldwide research interest and attention. Because of deep learning, AI technologies including speech, computer vision (CV), natural language progressing (NLP), and many others have progressed rapidly and even exceed human intelligence in some tasks. Their applications have been widely seen in the Internet, traffic, security, smart home, healthcare, and other industries.

Deep learning, a subfield of machine learning, differs from conventional machine learning methods in its ability to learn multiple levels of representation and abstraction by using several layers of nonlinear modules for feature extraction and transformation. Deep learning enables end-to-end training without the need of manually engineer features. With the help of big data, it significantly outperforms conventional methods. The extensive use and huge success of deep learning in speech, CV, and NLP have led to significant advances toward the full materialization of AI.

As one of the most active fields, deep learning is related to many aspects of AI industry developments. In China, because of the advantages in Internet, financial and human resources, market size, number of users, and massive amount of data, the country is becoming international market leadership in AI. Deep learning research and industrial applications are thriving and becoming increasingly popular and increasingly received by the public. In turn, they contribute to the research of fundamental theory, attracting business investments and talent.

This Blue Book focuses on the development of deep learning technologies. Global trends, deep learning development status in China and the future and discussion are presented in three chapters in this book.

Beijing, China   Center for Electronics and Information Studies,
                                                               Chinese Academy of Engineering

List of Series Contributors

The guidance group and working group of *Research on the Development of Electronic Information Engineering Technology in China* series are shown as below:

Guidance Group

Leader: Zuoning Chen, Xichen Lu

Member (In alphabetical order)**:**

Aiguo Fei, Baoyan Duan, Binxing Fang, Bohu Li, Changxiang Shen, Cheng Wu, Chengjun Wang, Chun Chen, Desen Yang, Dianyuan Fang, Endong Wang, Guangjun Zhang, Guangnan Ni, Guofan Jin, Guojie Li, Hao Dai, Hequan Wu, Huilin Jiang, Huixing Gong, Jiangxing Wu, Jianping Wu, Jiaxiong Fang, Jie Chen, Jiubin Tan, Jun Lu, Lianghui Chen, Manqing Wu, Qinping Zhao, Qionghai Dai, Shanghe Liu, Shaohua Yu, Tianchu Li, Tianran Wang, Tianyou Chai, Wen Gao, Wenhua Ding, Yu Wei, Yuanliang Ma, Yueguang Lv, Yueming Li, Zejin Liu, Zhijie Chen, Zhonghan Deng, Zhongqi Gao, Zishen Zhao, Zuyan Xu

Working Group

Leader: Shaohua Yu, Jun Lu

Deputy Leader: Da An, Meimei Dang, Shouren Xu

Member (In alphabetical order)**:**

Denian Shi, Dingyi Zhang, Fangfang Dai, Fei Dai, Fei Xing, Feng Zhou, Gang Qiao, Lan Zhou, Li Tao, Liang Chen, Lun Li, Mo Liu, Nan Meng, Peng Wang, Qiang Fu, Qingguo Wang, Rui Zhang, Shaohui Li, Wei He, Wei Xie, Xiangyang Ji, Xiaofeng Hu, Xingquan Zhang, Xiumei Shao, Yan Lu, Ying Wu, Yue Lu, Yunfeng Wei, Yuxiang Shu, Zheng Zheng, Zhigang Shang, Zhuang Liu

Contents

About the Authors

Chinese Academy of Engineering (CAE) is China's foremost academic and advisory institution in engineering and technological sciences, which has been enrolled in the first batch of pilot national high-end think tanks. As a national institution, CAE's missions are to study major strategic issues in economic and social development as well as in engineering technology progress and to build itself into a S&T think tank having significant influences on decision-making of national strategic issues. In today's world, the wave of information technologies featured by digitalization, networking, and intelligence is gaining momentum. Information technologies are experiencing rapid changes with each passing day and are fully applied in production and life, bringing about profound changes in global economic, political, and security landscapes. Among diverse information technologies, electronic information engineering technology is one of the most innovative and widely used technologies and plays its greatest role in driving the development of other S&T fields. In order to better carry out strategic studies on electronic information engineering technology, promote innovation in relevant systems and mechanisms and integrate superior resources, Center for Electronics and Information Studies (hereinafter referred to the "Center") was established in November 2015 by CAE in collaboration with Cyberspace Administration of China (CAC), the Ministry of Industry and Information Technology (MIIT), and China Electronics Technology Group Corporation (CETC).

The Center pursues high-level, open, and prospective development and is committed to conducting theoretical and application-oriented researches on cross-cutting, overarching, and strategically important hot topics concerning electronic information engineering technologies, and providing consultancy services for policymaking by brainstorming ideas from CAE academicians and experts and scholars from national ministries and commissions, businesses, public institutions, universities, and research institutions. The Center's mission is to build a top-notch strategic think tank that provides scientific, forward-looking, and timely advice for national policymaking in terms of electronic information engineering technology.

The main authors of *The Development of Deep Learning Technologies* are Haifeng Wang and Shaohua Yu.

Dr. Haifeng Wang is the first Chinese president in the history of ACL (Association for Computational Linguistics), the most influential international academic organization in the field of natural language processing, and the only ACL member from mainland China. In July 2018, he became the founding chairman of AACL of ACL Asia Pacific branch. He also holds various positions in a number of international academic organizations, international conferences, and international journals. He is the president and director of National Engineering Laboratory of deep learning technology and application. At the same time, he also served as vice president of China artificial intelligence industry development alliance, new generation artificial intelligence industry technology innovation strategy alliance, National Engineering Laboratory for brain-like intelligence technology and application, China Electronics Society, Chinese information society and other institutions, vice director of Technical Committee of National Engineering Laboratory for big data system software, and member of new generation artificial intelligence strategy advisory committee.

Dr. Shaohua Yu, Academician of Chinese Academy of Engineering(CAE), information and communication network technology expert. He is the chief engineer of China Information and Communication Technologies Group Co., Ltd., the chief engineer of China information and Communication Technology Group Co., Ltd., the director of State Key Laboratory of Optical Communication Technologies and Network, the vice president of China Institute of Communications, the member of national 863 Program Network and communication subject expert group, the member of cyber power strategy research advisory group, and the national integrated circuit industry development advisory committee Member. He has been engaged in the research of optical fiber communication and network technology for a long time, presided over and completed more than ten national projects such as 973 and 863, all of which have achieved transformation of achievements and a large number of applications. It is one of the pioneers of the integration of SDH (Synchronous Digital Hierarchy) and Internet (including Ethernet).

Chapter 1
Deep Learning: History and State-of-the-Arts

In recent years, deep learning has made an immense impact on both academia and industry. Many academic fields have witnessed deep learning-triggered breakthroughs and a rise in deep learning-related papers. Deep learning has become a buzzword at major academic conferences. Deep learning-related patents account for a sizable share of the AI patent applications. Meanwhile, industrial advancements and new products due to deep learning have greatly changed our manner of working, studying, and living. Widely used in a variety of important fields, deep learning has empowered increasing numbers of applications in information retrieval, information exchange, shopping, healthcare, finance, and industrial manufacturing, which undoubtedly will become increasingly important in our daily lives in the future.

1.1 An Overview of Deep Learning

1.1.1 The History of Deep Learning

Although popular in recent years, deep learning did not evolve overnight. It has a long history.

Currently, the mainstream deep learning approaches are based on neural networks that have been researched for decades with varying levels of success.

The idea of neural networks originated in 1943. Walter Pitts, an American mathematician and logician, and Warren McCulloch, a psychologist, published their paper, "A Logical Calculus of the Ideas Immanent in Nervous Activity," proposing a mathematical formalization of neural activities and a model of neural networks.

In 1958, Frank Rosenblatt, a professor at Cornell University, built the two-layer perceptron, an artificial neural network model trained using Hebb's learning rule or

© China Science Publishing & Media Ltd (Science Press) 2020
Center for Electronics and Information Studies, Chinese Academy
of Engineering, *The Development of Deep Learning Technologies*,
https://doi.org/10.1007/978-981-15-4584-9_1

least-squares method. The perceptron inspired a great many scientists' interests in artificial neural networks.

In 1969, Marvin Minsky and Seymour Papert, coinventors of the Logo programming language, presented a number of mathematical proofs characterizing various limitations of the single-layer perceptron. For example, it is incapable of solving the Exclusive Or (XOR) problem. Then, artificial neural networks became less popular in the 1970s.

It was not until 1986 when David Rumelhart, Geoffrey Hinton, and Ronald Williams reproposed the back-propagation algorithm and applied it to multilayer neural networks that the second wave of neural network research emerged.

In 1989, Robert Hecht-Nielsen proved the universal approximation theorem of the multilayer perceptron (MLP). The same year, Yann LeCun proposed the convolutional neural network (CNN), a commonly used deep learning model, and successfully applied it to the task of recognizing handwritten digits.

Unfortunately, computers were very slow in the 1980s, making it barely possible to train deep networks. In addition, when training with back-propagation, scaling up the neural network led to the vanishing gradient problem, which limited progress in neural network research as well as applications. When shallow learning algorithms, such as support vector machine (SVM), were proposed in the 1990s and outperformed neural networks on classification and regression problems, interest in neural network research declined once again.

The year 2006 is considered the start of deep learning, when Geoffrey Hinton and his student Ruslan Salakhutdinov initially coined the term deep learning [1]. Their paper published in the journal Science gave a detailed solution to the vanishing gradient problem—layer-by-layer unsupervised learning followed by fine-tuning via supervised back-propagation. This paper brought attention back to deep neural networks (DNN).

Then, the rapid progress of computer hardware, especially the huge advance and wide use of GPUs, dramatically enhanced computing power and made it possible to use complicated compound nonlinear functions to learn the distributed and hierarchical feature representations. Additionally, the Internet brought about massive data. Machine learning with big data received increasing recognition from industry, which stimulated its further development.

In approximately 2011, Geoffrey Hinton and Microsoft's researchers applied deep learning to speech recognition and achieved a significant milestone. In 2012, Geoffrey Hinton and his team won the ImageNet Large Scale Visual Recognition Challenge (ILSVRC) with their deep learning model AlexNet [2], reducing the error rate from 26 to 15%.

Deep learning's breakthroughs in speech and image tasks have attracted great attention from academia and industry and opened the floodgates of deep learning research and applications. During the following years, there was significant work performed concerning deep learning algorithms and model research, programming framework construction, training acceleration, and application extension. New breakthroughs blossomed in a wider range of fields and began to have social and economic effects.

It is worth mentioning that deep learning's historic performance on computer-based Go was so interesting and astonishing that it made the concept of deep learning and AI known to the public and their research and applications more accepted by society.

In 2016, AlphaGo, developed based on deep learning by Google DeepMind, shocked the world with a 4-1 victory against Lee Sedol, a South Korean professional Go player of 9 dan rank and the Go World Champion. Subsequently, it continued to win against other Go grandmasters, which marks the deep learning-based AI Go player's triumph over humans.

In 2017, AlphaGo evolved to AlphaGo Zero. Using no data from human games, it started from zero and independently became a master. After playing games against itself for 3 days, it defeated AlphaGo in a 100-game match by 100 to 0.

AlphaGo and AlphaGo Zero used a combination of deep learning and reinforcement learning. The former is good at perception, while the latter focuses on decision-making. AlphaGo combined deep learning and a Monte Carlo tree search and used two networks to improve search efficiency—one policy network to select moves and reduce search breadth, and one value network to evaluate board positions and reduce search depth. In this manner, AlphaGo was able to determine the move that has the highest probability of winning at each step in a far more efficient and accurate manner. The policy network was trained through self-playing reinforcement learning, while the value network was trained using data generated by the self-playing and rapid rollout. In the game, the policy and value networks are combined with a Monte Carlo tree search to select the best move at each position.

AlphaGo Zero, the upgraded version, merged the policy and value networks into one and learned from end-to-end self-play reinforcement learning. The champion-defeating AlphaGo was trained using a large amount of human game data and manual feature design, while AlphaGo Zero was trained solely by self-play learning from a randomly initialized network, achieving higher performance in a shorter time and with fewer resources. AlphaGo Zero's success is mainly driven by the better use of deep neural networks. Using a deeper residual network allows it to take the raw board positions as input in more complex games. Combining the separate policy and value networks into a single unified network results in more efficient training and better performance. Overall, the architecture of AlphaGo Zero is simpler and unified, yet powerful.

AlphaGo and AlphaGo Zero's conquering of the game of Go, the most complicated and ever-changing board game, has demonstrated the power of the combination of deep learning and reinforcement learning, and helped to popularize deep learning among the general public.

1.1.2   Academic Research

Deep Learning has become a focus of academic research. As evidenced by a surge of related papers, deep learning has become a major topic at international academic conferences. Over the past few years, there has been a vigorous growth in the

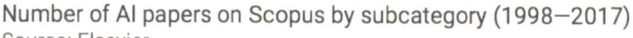

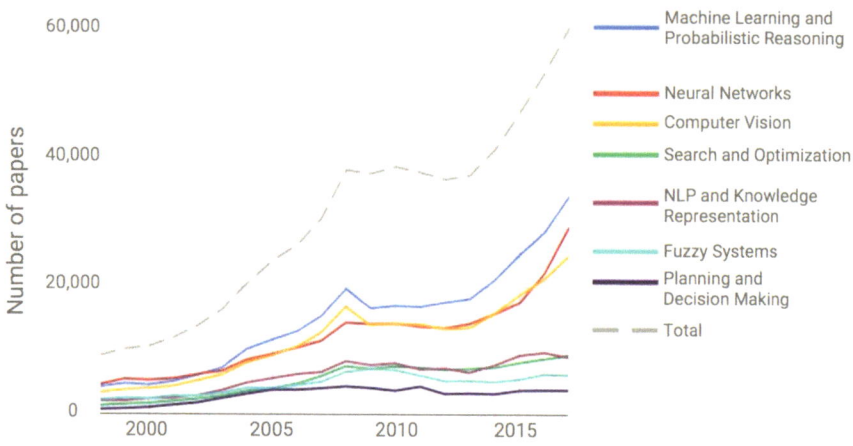

Fig. 1.1 The numbers of AI-related papers on Scopus between 1998 and 2017

number of academic publications relating to AI. The increase in papers on deep learning and its application is particularly impressive. According to Stanford's *Artificial Intelligence Index 2018 Annual Report*, 28% of published papers were in the Machine Learning and Probabilistic Reasoning category in 2010, while the percentage rose to 56% in 2017. Moreover, the number of papers in the Neural Networks category grew at a compound annual growth rate (CAGR) of 37% between 2014 and 2017, compared with the CAGR of 3% between 2010 and 2014 [3]. The numbers of AI-related papers on Scopus between 1998 and 2017 are shown by subcategory in Fig. 1.1.

Based on the increasing number of papers submitted to and accepted by international conferences in recent years, deep learning is currently one of the most popular research topics. Deep learning has become a central theme in highly selective top-ranked conferences such as the International Conference on Machine Learning (ICML), Conference on Neural Information Processing Systems (NeurIPS), Association for the Advancement of Artificial Intelligence (AAAI), International Joint Conference on Artificial Intelligence (IJCAI), and Association for Computational Linguistics (ACL) conferences.

Patents also show a steep increase in deep learning-related work. Recently, with the rapid development of AI technologies and industry, there has been a rapid increase in the number of AI patents being filed; the majority are in the field of deep learning.

A report from EconSight asserts that machine learning has dominated the AI patent landscape, ahead of other categories including deep learning and neural networks. The growth in deep learning-related patent filings is especially impressive [4], as shown in Fig. 1.2.

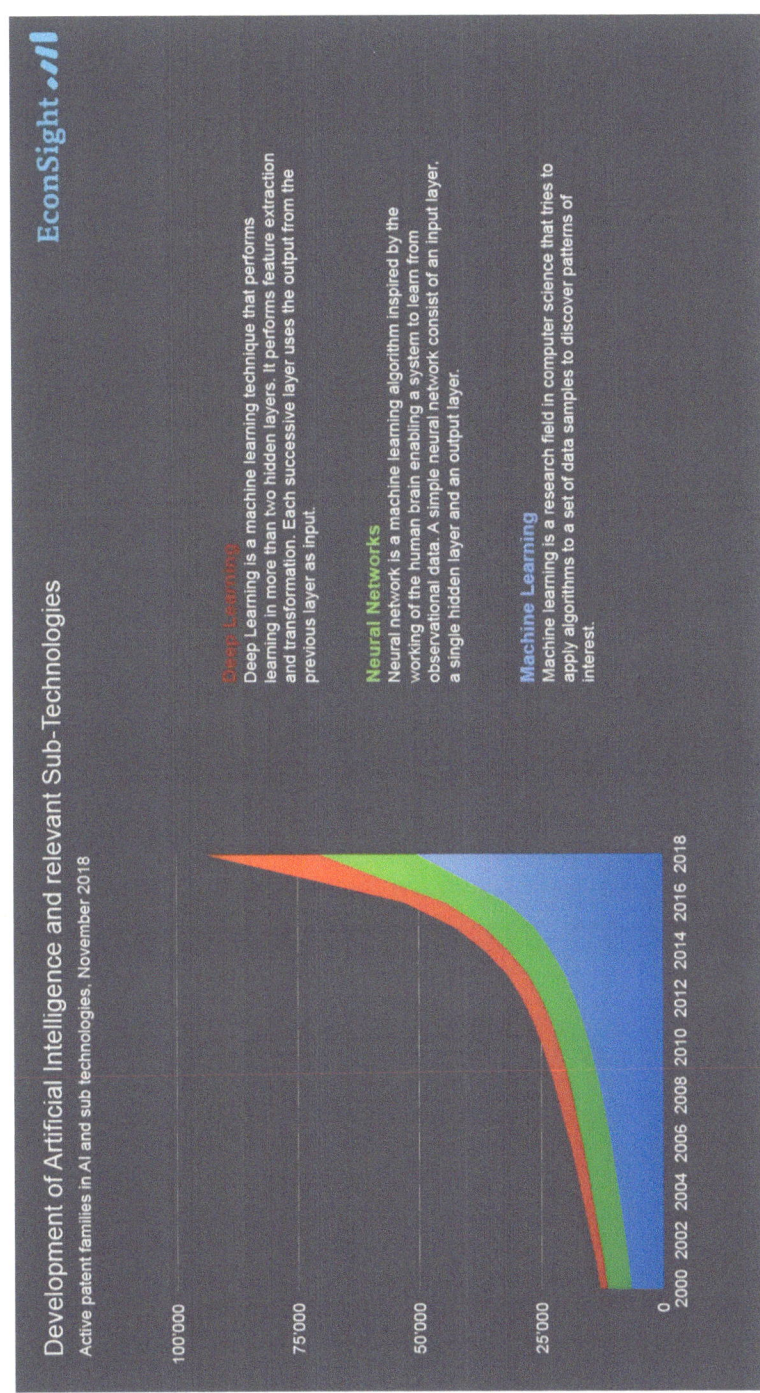

Fig. 1.2 The growth in deep learning-related patent

Moreover, *WIPO Technology Trends 2019: Artificial Intelligence*, published by the UN World Intellectual Property Organization (WIPO), mentions that nearly 340,000 AI-related patent applications were filed through the end of 2016, and more than half of them were made after 2013 [5]. Deep learning, the most popular AI technology in terms of patent filings, showed an average annual growth rate of 174.6% between 2013 and 2016.

1.1.3 Applied Technologies

The breakthroughs in deep learning and cloud computing have led to significant improvements in AI technologies including speech, computer vision, and natural language processing. AI-related products are suddenly appearing worldwide.

1.1.3.1 Speech Recognition

Driven by deep learning, speech recognition accuracy continues to improve, approaching, or even surpassing human capabilities (under ideal low-noise conditions). In recent years, traditional approaches to speech recognition such as Hidden Markov Models and Gaussian Mixture Models (HMM-GMM) are being replaced with more modern end-to-end systems. In January 2019, the Chinese company Baidu announced the Streaming Multi-Layer Truncated Attention Model (SMLTA), a major milestone in large-scale deployment of an attention model in an online speech recognition service. Compared to the previous connectionist temporal classification (CTC) system, SMLTA increased the online speech recognition accuracy by 15%. In addition, the following two features further enhance the user experience: (1) support for offline input and (2) support for code-switching (i.e., input consisting of mixed-language combinations of both Chinese and English, often in the same sentence).

1.1.3.2 Image Recognition

OpenCV, an open-source computer vision software library, has made a major contribution to the development of image recognition. OpenCV contains a deep learning sublibrary. Deep learning has distinct advantages over traditional machine learning methods in general, and especially for image recognition. For example, AlexNet, which is based on a deep convolutional neural network, was the winner of the ILSVRC 2012 and achieved a top-five error rate of 15.3%. Since then, deep CNNs have continued to perform well. All types of deep learning-based image recognition products have emerged and are widely used in numerous fields.

1.1.3.3   Natural Language Processing

NLP is a field long dominated by conventional machine learning, where neural networks have received little attention for a variety of reasons. Deep learning-based NLP research starts from neural network language models and word embeddings. Deep learning-based word embeddings have brought new approaches for general semantic representation and computation, improved various tasks including question answering and semantic matching, and facilitated multitask learning and transfer learning in NLP. Neural machine translation (NMT), which is based on deep learning, is one of the most significant breakthroughs in NLP. It outperforms statistic machine translation with simpler systems. Practical applications of NMT have been greatly promoted. Products such as portable translation machines have been developed. In addition, deep learning has driven the progress in new areas such as machine reading comprehension. However, natural language understanding remains a very difficult problem. NLP remains a field where deep learning has an important role in the future.

1.1.3.4   Data Intelligence

There has been considerable progress in recent years in both the theory and practice of deep learning. Recent advances in GPU hardening make it increasingly feasible to take advantage of big data. China's large AI companies are taking advantage of big data to build smart cities. This work involves finance, law, communication, transportation, security defense, and other areas critical to national welfare and people's livelihoods. For enterprises, deep learning has greatly facilitated the big data-driven applications such as search, advertisements, and user portraits.

1.2   Deep Learning in Industries

1.2.1   The Increasing Global Market

An important driving factor for deep learning market growth is the progress of AI chipsets. Currently, graphics processing units (GPUs) and central processing units (CPUs) dominate the market, but field-programmable gate arrays (FPGAs), application-specific integrated circuits (ASICs), system-on-a-chip (SoC) accelerators, and other emerging chipsets are becoming increasingly important. Although the market for deep learning chipsets is quite new, the landscape is changing quickly. In the past year, more than 60 companies, both large and small have announced a variety of deep learning hardware designs and/or chipsets. According to Tractica, 2019 and 2020 will be critical years when volumes increase significantly and future market leaders begin to emerge. By 2025, SoC accelerators will dominate the

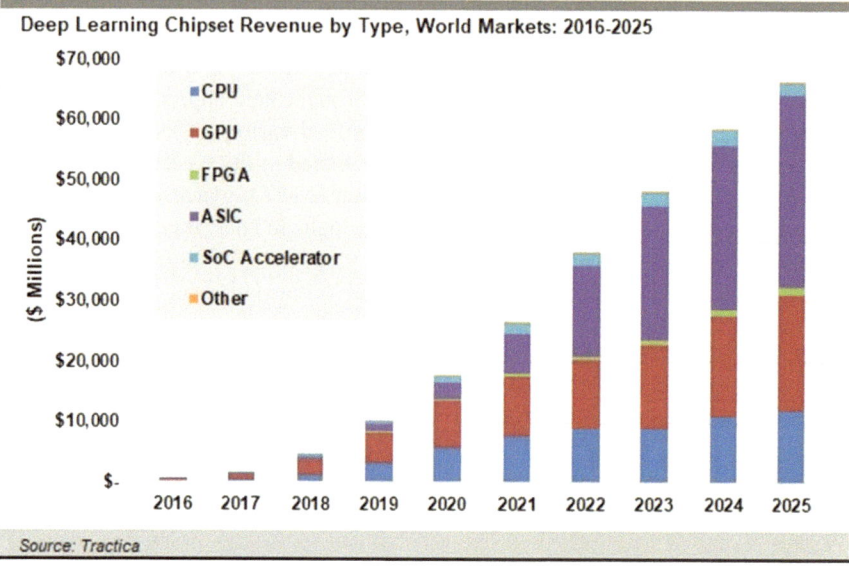

Fig. 1.3 Deep learning chipset revenue by type

market in terms of sheer volume, followed by ASICs and GPUs. In terms of revenue, the ASICs will dominate the market in 2025, followed by GPUs and CPUs, as illustrated in Fig. 1.3.

Artificial intelligence computing today is mostly performed in cloud data centers. According to a recent report from Tractica, however, with increasing diversity of AI applications, an increasing amount of AI computing will move to edge devices. Mobile phones will become the dominant force in the edge computing market, followed by a number of other important edge devices such as smart speakers, PCs/tablets, head-mounted displays, automobiles, drones, consumer and enterprise robots, and security cameras.

To date, deep learning has made major contributions to a variety of fields such as image recognition, text analysis, product recommendation, fraud prevention, and content management. In the future, deep learning is likely to facilitate the development of more powerful and groundbreaking applications, such as autonomous cars, personalized education, and preventative healthcare. As Tractica forecasts [6], the global market of deep learning software will grow to $67.2 billion USD by 2025, as shown in Fig. 1.4. There are great opportunities for deep learning across a wide array of industries and geographic areas, especially in those highly domain-specific markets that can benefit from deep learning's advantages of big data, machine perception, and others.

The deep learning markets in North America and Asia Pacific are currently growing very quickly. According to a report from Persistence Market Research [7], 40%

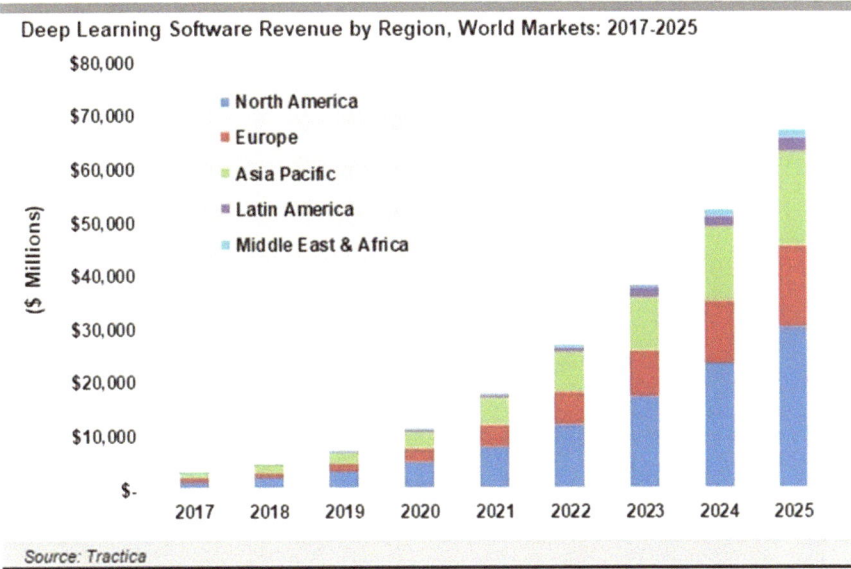

Fig. 1.4 Deep learning software revenue by region

of the deep learning market will be in North America by 2027. The Asia Pacific deep learning market is expected to be one of the key regional markets to generate sustainable revenue in the next 2 years.

1.2.2 Industrial Applications

Deep learning has been rapidly applied to many areas over the past few years. Deep learning chipsets in cloud and terminal devices have also been widely used, producing a number of products in information services, shopping, security, finance, transportation, home applications, automobile, and other industries. According to the Gartner Hype Cycle in 2018, presented in Fig. 1.5, deep learning and deep neural network ASICs are gaining traction quickly and are expected to reach mainstream adoption in the next 2–5 years [8].

Currently, Facebook uses CNNs for its photo tagging and face detection. In the field of intelligent vehicles, Tesla's Model X uses CNNs for its self-driving feature.

In the healthcare industry, companies such as Quere.ai are using CNNs and achieving notable success in prognosis and diagnosis with medical imaging. In addition, GPU-accelerated deep learning solutions are used to develop intricate neural networks for medical and healthcare applications, such as real-time pathology assessment, point-of-care interventions, and predictive analytics for clinical

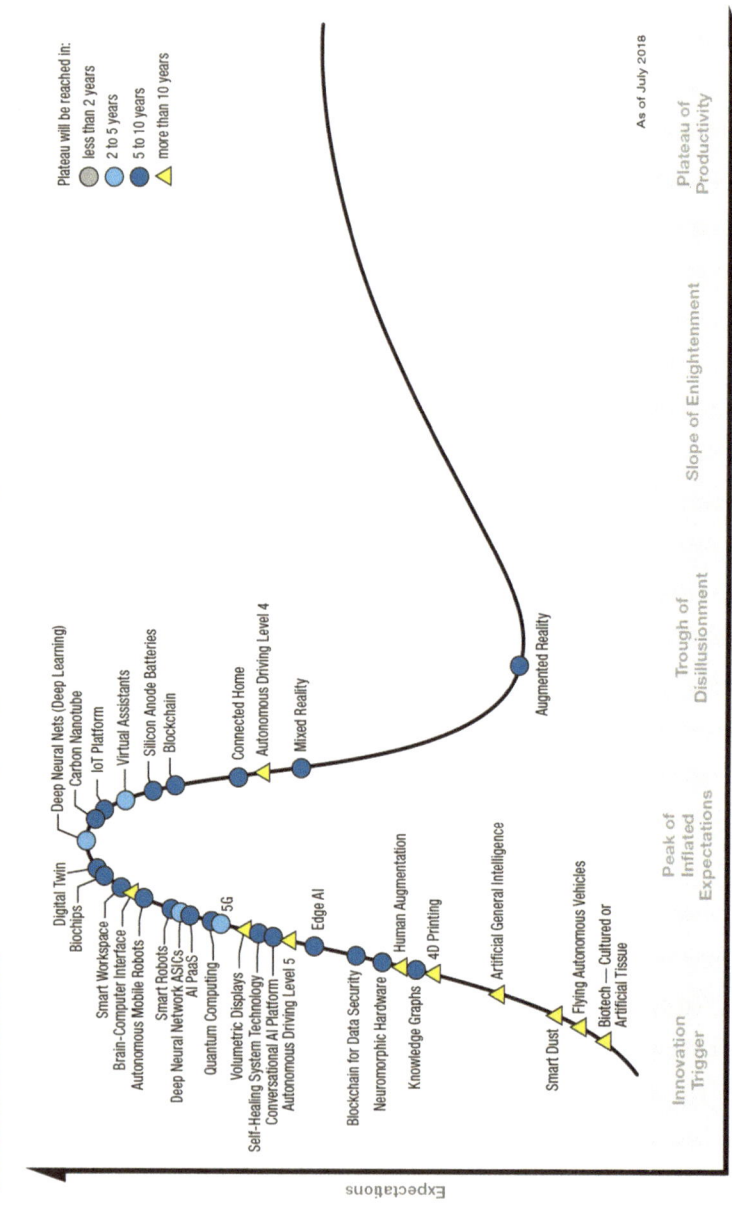

Fig. 1.5 Deep learning and deep neural network ASICs

decision-making. Innovations in deep learning are producing unbelievable progress in precision medicine and population health management (PHM).

In financial investment, virtual assistants based on deep learning have begun to assume the work of human consultants. In the United States, not only are high-technology companies such as Betterment and Wealth Front engaging in intelligent consulting, but AI is also influencing traditional financial organizations. Goldman Sachs acquired Honest Dollar and BlackRock acquired FutureAdvisor. The Royal Bank of Scotland has announced it will deploy an AI virtual assistant to replace hundreds of human advisors. Some Chinese startup companies are attempting to use AI technologies in the insurance industry, developing knowledge graphs based on insurance databases and collecting more data for AI question answering services. With a growing number of organizations embracing AI assistants, it is possible that the number of virtual assistants could come close to the human level in the next 2–5 years.

Deep learning is reducing costs, both labor costs and the cost of machinery. Deep learning algorithms can improve themselves with no need for additional data, increasing efficiency, and decreasing costs. For example, when applied to industrial machinery, deep learning algorithms help detect product defects that would have otherwise been very difficult to detect. Deep networks are particularly good at addressing real-world challenges such as noisy images due to environmental conditions, product reflection, and lens distortion. Addressing these realities more effectively makes inspection more robust and efficient.

Although deep learning-based AI technologies have shown great potential and even surpassed human abilities in some areas, deep learning is not without its limitations. In particular, it performs well on perception tasks, but not so well on cognitive tasks requiring knowledge and/or understanding. Supervised learning is more effective than unsupervised learning. There is no data like more data. Deep learning is more effective when there is plenty of training data, though pretrained models make it feasible to fine-tune a model based on big data to a use case where data are not as plentiful. In addition, neural networks require manually designed architectures, though there are some attempts to automate this process. Automated architecture search is mostly used to fine-tune local networks; expert design is still required for most cases.

Although limited, deep learning is still believed to be at the heart of the future of the industry as improvements in algorithms, computing power, tools, and all types of applications will constantly advance the development of software, hardware, deep learning frameworks, and AI chipsets.

Chapter 2
Deep Learning Development Status in China

2.1 An Overview

In the new wave of technological revolution driven by deep learning, China is pioneering in the field of applied technology at "China speed," but is relatively underdeveloped in fundamental theories and lower level technologies.

2.1.1 Fundamental Theory and Lower Level Technologies

High-end chips are central in powering AI and deep learning algorithms. According to World Semiconductor Trade Statistics (WSTS), the global semiconductor market had an output value of $468.8 billion USD in 2018. The Chinese revenue was less than $40 billion USD, accounting for a relatively small market share of just 8%. On the demand side, semiconductor consumption in China exceeded $150 billion USD, accounting for 34% of the global market. There is clearly a large trade imbalance; 26% of the demand is imported. Since 2015, a great number of AI chip-related startup companies have launched in China. The first among these is Cambricon Technologies, a company designing AI chips for both edge processing and cloud computing. Its neural processing unit (NPU) chip series 1A/1H was integrated into Hisilicon Kirin 970/980 chipsets, delivering high performance to Huawei's flagship smartphones. Meanwhile, China's large technical companies such as Alibaba and Baidu are also in the AI chip business. They are conducting research and developing their own AI chips, as well as investing in startup companies. Alibaba launched a neural network chip called Ali-NPU for AI inference in 2018. Baidu successively released two AI chips in 2018 and 2019, the general-purpose cloud AI chip, Kunlun, and the specialized AI chip, Honghu, designed for far-field voice interaction.

Deep learning frameworks are another fundamental technology accelerating AI research and applications. In 2010, the world's first deep learning framework,

© China Science Publishing & Media Ltd (Science Press) 2020
Center for Electronics and Information Studies, Chinese Academy
of Engineering, *The Development of Deep Learning Technologies*,
https://doi.org/10.1007/978-981-15-4584-9_2

Theano, was introduced and open-sourced by the University of Montreal. Subsequently, many technical companies around the world announced their deep learning toolkits, including Google's TensorFlow, the most commonly used deep learning platform today; Facebook's PyTorch and Caffe2, fast-growing deep learning tools; the Microsoft Cognitive Toolkit (CNTK); and so on. In 2016, Baidu unveiled PaddlePaddle, China's first open-source deep learning platform that integrates end-to-end frameworks for both parallel distributed training and highly efficient inference. PaddlePaddle also provides pretrained models, convenient tools, and flexible services for customized deployments and management, useful features for a broad range of business scenarios. The concept of deep learning and underlying theories are primarily proposed by researchers in the United States and Canada; however, the gap is closing. There has been some recent encouraging progress in China in fundamental theory and lower level technologies.

2.1.2 Applied Technologies

The term "China speed" describes the rapid rate of development in China, especially in applied technologies. There are three driving forces behind "China speed": (1) infrastructure, (2) data, and (3) funding.

First, the infrastructure in China is based on the well-established Internet industry, led by the key players Baidu, Alibaba, and Tencent (BAT). Second, data are a huge advantage for China, given the scale of the Chinese market. There are 829 million Internet users in China who generate trillions of data records daily. This advantage in data will fuel all types of machine learning innovations. Third, funding opportunities in China are good and improving. According to a CB Insights report, China's AI startup companies raised 48% of global funding in 2017, surpassing those in the United States for the first time.

In China, innovations in deep learning occur on multiple fronts. Currently, deep learning is especially popular in speech recognition and computer vision. Deep learning is also important in natural language processing, especially in the subfield of machine translation. There are international competitions in many of these areas. China has been making dramatic progress, as seen in these competitions, especially in computer vision. In particular, all of the ILSVRC 2016 tracks were won by a team from China. These teams are affiliated with SenseTime, Hikvision, the Chinese University of Hong Kong (CUHK), City University of Hong Kong (CityU), and Nanjing University of Information Science & Technology (NUIST).

Other teams from China have done well in other competitions. A team from Baidu won the 2018 WebVision Challenge, a large-scale visual recognition contest. As announced by the National Institute of Standards and Technology (NIST) on November 16, 2018, the top five teams in a Face Recognition Vendor Test (FRVT) include two Chinese AI startup companies, YITU and SenseTime, as well as the Shenzhen Institute of Advanced Technology (SIAT) of the Chinese Academy of Sciences (CAS). In January 2019, the VIM-FD algorithm proposed by Vimicro broke the record with a score of 0.967 in the WIDER Face and Person Challenge. In the field of computer Go, Tecent's version of AlphaGo, Fine Art, defeated Japanese Go AI, DeepZenGo, in 2017, and became the official training bot for the Chinese national Go team in 2018.

2.1.3   Industrial Applications

Currently, deep learning-based AI technologies have been widely applied to many industries in China. High-technology companies such as BAT use deep learning in their key products. They are also building open platforms to make AI capabilities more available to everyone. Startup companies are developing deep learning applications in vertical markets, such as intelligent finance, security, education, healthcare, and so forth.

Increasing numbers of commercial products are using increasing amounts of deep learning. Such products include smart speakers equipped with speech input and output and security cameras equipped with face recognition. Face recognition has already been widely deployed in airports, railway stations, and banks. As mentioned above, deep learning has made significant contributions to machine translation, and machine translation products are becoming increasingly practical. We are now beginning to see some products that support simultaneous interpretation (i.e., speech-to-speech translation with no need to slow down the conversation to wait for the translation). Computer-aided medical diagnosis systems help doctors make better-informed diagnoses by summarizing information from medical imaging, test results, and patient medical histories.

Deep learning-based AI technologies are changing the world. AI-driven applications are becoming ubiquitous. With the continuous evolution of AI technology, China is welcoming a new era of industrial intelligence.

2.2   The Kernel Technologies

2.2.1   AI Chips

2.2.1.1   Current Development of AI Chips

China is in a state of catching up in the IC industry, especially in the field of computer core chips such as CPUs. United States and European companies hold much of the Core IC technology and intellectual property. Although progress had been increasing dramatically, the technology may soon reach fundamental limits due to physics. This is especially the case for well-studied chips such as CPUs. On the other hand, there may be more opportunities for deep learning chips, where China is not as far behind; therefore, there may be some opportunities for China to make

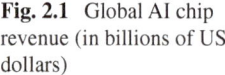

Fig. 2.1 Global AI chip revenue (in billions of US dollars)

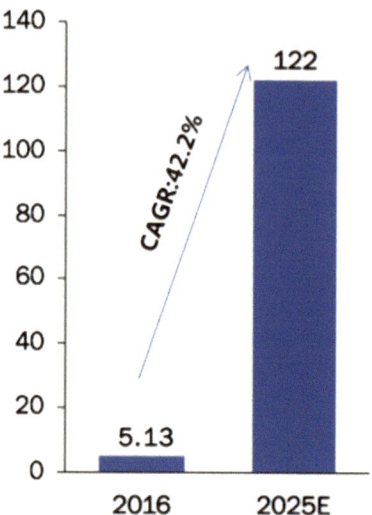

gains in IC manufacturing. Among them, deep learning frameworks and AI chips will play a vital role. Hardware foundations such as AI chips are the core of the computing resource that AI needs, while deep learning frameworks are the operating systems in the AI era. A plausible way to catch up is to invest in research and development, focusing on combinations of AI chips and deep learning frameworks. These investments will create a fully integrated system of software and hardware that supports the entire process from algorithms to training and ultimately deployment in industrial applications. The end goal is to build a complete AI technology ecosystem.

The AI chip market shows strong growth because of the artificial intelligence boom. According to Tractica's forecast, as shown in Fig. 2.1, the AI chip revenue will increase from $513 million USD (approximately 3.4 billion yuan) in 2016 to $12.2 billion USD (approximately 81.3 billion yuan) in 2025, with a compound annual growth rate of 42.2%. The annual AI chip shipments will increase from 863,000 in 2016 to 41.2 million in 2025, as shown in Fig. 2.2. By comparison, GPUs, which are more suitable for large-scale parallel computing, and ASICs for deep learning show much faster growth and much higher proportion than traditional CPUs.

2.2.1.2   Deep Learning Compatible AI Chip Technology

AI chips and deep learning frameworks are interdependent core elements of the ever-developing artificial intelligence industry. Both chips and frameworks bridge the gap between networks and solutions. Deep learning frameworks translate deep neural networks into executable instructions on chips. AI chips elevate the performance of frameworks by providing instruction sets, optimized for AI applications.

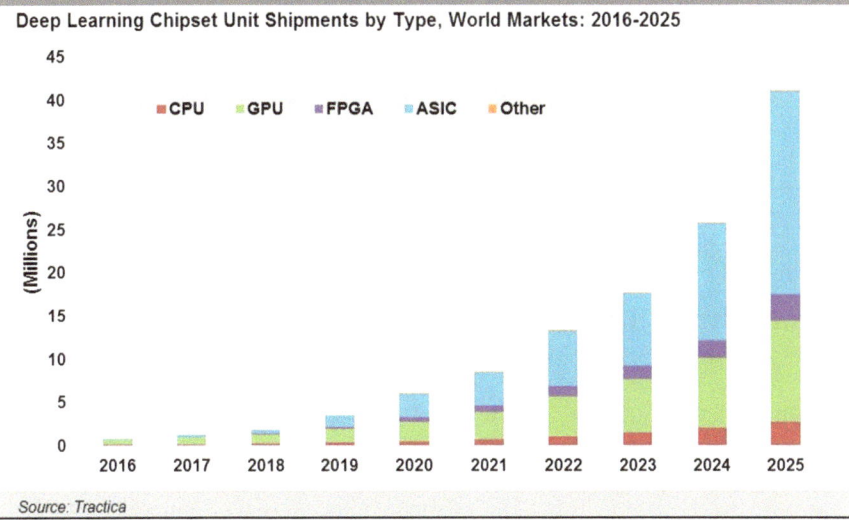

Fig. 2.2 Deep learning chipset unit shipments by type

Broadly speaking, AI chips empower AI programs. Evaluating the details, deep learning involves the two phases of training and inference. The two phases have very different hardware requirements; therefore, it is likely that the industry will develop different chips for the different phases.

Training makes use of a significant amount of resources (big data) and a significant amount of computing power (matrix multiplication). Matrix multiplication is often used during training to fit model parameters using gradient descent (or one of its variants). GPUs tend to be better than CPUs for multiplying these types of matrices because GPUs have more opportunities to take advantage of parallelism. GPUs have thousands of compute cores and additional high-speed memory.

There are a number of hardware designs that might be helpful for training, including GPUs, FPGAs, ASICs, and clusters. FPGAs are programmable logic devices that can be reprogrammed after manufacturing according to the functionality requirements of the deep learning algorithms. Google's TPU is a type of ASIC chip. ASICs are specially configured for particular applications, with instruction sets, microstructures, artificial neural circuits, and memory systems that are configurable for deep learning algorithms. Most AI enterprises are currently using large clusters of GPUs and/or TPUs.

Inference is very different from training. Inference takes the trained model as input and makes a prediction based on real-world data. Inference requires less computation than training, but it may require more resources (i.e., compute, memory, and power) than what is available at the edge (i.e., on a phone or in a smart speaker). Thus, some applications choose to upload data to the cloud, run inference on the cloud, and return the results to the edge in real time. Since the cloud will likely support many users in parallel, there are considerable opportunities for high-performance cloud AI chips to support inference, especially in cloud-based designs. These designs can supply huge numbers of simultaneous computations, as required by many AI applications such as machine translation and identity verification. These applications need to process large quantities of photos, audio, video, natural language, and other inputs.

There are also hardware opportunities for edge-based designs. Edge-based designs are attractive for tasks with ultrahigh speed requirements and/or low-power requirements, as well as for tasks that need to work with and without Internet connections. Unlike cloud chips, edge-based AI chips are embedded in small devices with severe constraints on size, power, and weight and provide a lightweight software environment. Edge-based solutions do not need to be as powerful as cloud-based solutions because edge-based solutions do not need to support as many simultaneous users and services. Edge-based solutions normally support only one or two AI functions. Currently, most mobile phones and cameras are beginning to take advantage of edge-based AI chips.

Currently, AI chips, including CPUs, GPUs, FPGAs, and ASICs, continue to have various shortcomings in terms of adaptability, power consumption, and performance. Deep learning algorithms and frameworks are evolving relatively quickly compared to hardware. The design and development cycles of chips are generally longer than the software design and development cycles. Consequently, chip solutions are appropriate for relatively mature algorithms, but probably not for algorithms that are unlikely to persist.

In summary, AI chips are evolving to have the following characteristics:

1. Synergy with deep learning frameworks. The combination of deep learning frameworks and AI chips is one of the key points of building an entire AI hardware and software ecosystem. The vast majority of artificial intelligence applications are powered by deep learning. Most of these applications are based on deep learning frameworks, which are closely tied to particular AI chips. Optimizations at the chip and instruction set levels are needed to obtain competitive efficiency and performance.

2. Flexibility. Traditionally, general-purpose hardware designs tend to survive better than special-purpose solutions. This same trend applies to AI chips because deep learning algorithms are constantly improving. AI chips need to be flexible enough to cope with the diversity and rapid evolution of new and improved deep learning algorithms. That is, AI chips need to be architecturally reconfigurable or self-learning instead of following predesigned algorithms during training or implementation.

3. High-computing power and programmable capacity. AI chips should be programmable and have high-efficiency and low-consumption computing power to maintain pace with the rapid development of deep learning algorithms and various applications.

4. High performance and small size. AI chips, although small, must provide high performance under low-power requirements. The challenge is to deliver stable

and reliable service in a variety of portable devices and a variety of scenarios, such as consumer electronics, healthcare, education, logistics, and security.

5. Easy-to-use tools for AI chip development. AI chips require massive parallelism, making it difficult to design AI chips. The chip design process can be time-consuming. Demand for customized AI chips exceeds supply, making it difficult to set priorities. Scheduling limited resources would be easier if we could increase the AI chip supply by making it easier to develop more chips more quickly. Better (i.e., easier to use) tools will make it possible for more people to contribute to future chip designs. Today's tools require too much knowledge of the chip design process, limiting the number of potential developers, and consequently, limiting the quality and quantity of AI chips.

2.2.1.3   Diversified Applications of AI Chips

According to application scenarios, AI chips can be divided into two types of (1) cloud and (2) edge. The two types have very different requirements. Power and cost are important in both cases, but power and cost constraints tend to be more severe for the edge. There are many examples of potential applications for AI chips in both the cloud and the edge. Almost every public cloud service provider deploys high-performance cloud computing servers for video encoding and decoding, deep learning, scientific computing, and other fields. Many of these functions can also be performed on edge and Internet of Things (IoT) devices, including smartphones, advanced driver assistance systems (ADAS), smart cameras, voice interaction devices, VR/AR equipment, and other devices.

1. Cloud data center. Cloud AI chips, which are characterized by powerful performance, can support a large number of operations simultaneously and can flexibly support image, voice, video processing, and other AI applications. Large companies around the world are competing in this huge market. In China, large high-technology companies such as Baidu, Alibaba, Tencent, and iFlytek have entered the field of cloud AI chips; however, to date, most of these investments have not produced large returns. In August 2017, Baidu released the 256 core FPGA-based cloud AI chip XPU and in July 2018 announced its cloud-to-edge AI chip Kunlun.

2. Security. Security is one of the fields in which AI chips are most widely used. More than 80% of Chinese AI chip startup companies are participating in the security market. The AI security chip market is developing rapidly as the potential of the security industry becomes clear. Recently, there has been rapid growth in interprocessing communication (IPC) SoC chips for products such as the Huawei HiSilicon. Vimicro has also released an embedded neural network processor (NPU) chip. This deep learning-based chip is used in face recognition; its accuracy is better than a human eye. In May 2018, Cambricon released the cloud AI chip MLU100, which features 80 W board power consumption and 110 W peak power consumption. This chip supports balance and high-performance modes.

3. Home/consumer electronics. In the Artificial Intelligence + Internet of Things (AIoT), all devices will be interconnected, forming a new ecosystem of data interaction and sharing. In this process, edge devices must support autonomous local decision-making with limited computational power. Many products in the smart home industry support voice interaction. Devices in the home are expected to recognize and understand user commands, a challenging requirement for edge computing. Various AI technologies are common in the consumer electronics industry. Face recognition is often used to unlock smartphones and verify mobile payments. Beauty cameras optimize images to look better than reality. In September 2018, Huawei released its AI chip Kirin 980, which is equipped with an optimized version of Cambrian 1A and uses a dual-core structure. Its image recognition speed is greatly improved to 4500 images per minute. It also supports multiperson real-time gesture recognition and real-time video background replacement. In addition to image processing, the Kirin 980 has a three-level energy-efficiency architecture that has several sets of cores and uses the flex-scheduling mechanism to intelligently distribute the cores for heavy, medium, and light load scenarios. The super cores are intended for games, large cores for social communication, and small cores for music.

4. Autonomous driving. NVIDIA, Intel, and various startup companies are producing AI chips that are becoming core components of autonomous driving computing platforms. From a technical point of view, autonomous driving chips adopt the same hardware technologies as deep learning, i.e., GPU, FPGA, and ASIC. According to the levels of automation released by SAE International, commercial autonomous driving chips are currently found as part of ADAS, supporting L1 assisted driving and L2 partial automated driving. AI chips for L4 high automated driving and L5 full automated driving are far from large-scale commercial use. Chinese startup company Fabu Technology developed a 28-nm-deep learning accelerator based on its self-designed MPV architecture, which supports a variety of sensors such as cameras, laser radar, and millimeter-wave radar and enables real-time high accuracy 3D environment sensing. It has an operating frequency of over 1 GHz and offers computing power of over 4TOPs. Breakthroughs were also made in its power consumption, cost, and other key indicators, enabling it to fully support L3/L4 real-time data processing.

In addition to security, home/consumer electronics, autonomous driving, and cloud computing, AI chips will have new growth opportunities in education, healthcare, manufacturing, and other industries.

2.2.2 Deep Learning Framework

Artificial intelligence chips and deep learning frameworks are the two most fundamental infrastructures in the deep learning area and play a vital role in the development of the AI industry. The deep learning framework has become a vital tool of AI researchers and developers who focus on AI research and application development.

2.2.2.1 Current Development of Deep Learning Frameworks

Deep learning frameworks are becoming more modular. One of the first frameworks, Theano, was open-sourced by the University of Montreal in 2010. Soon thereafter, UC Berkeley open-sourced Caffe, which was designed for computer vision applications. Since then, technology companies have taken the lead in research and development of deep learning frameworks. Many of these frameworks are distributed as open-source. For example, Google released TensorFlow in 2015, Baidu released PaddlePaddle in 2016, and Facebook released Pytorch in 2017. Caffe was initially designed for computer vision-based deep learning algorithms, with comprehensive prototyping of various computer vision algorithms; it has been used prevalently in the area of computer vision. TensorFlow supports large-scale parallel computing, based on a computation graph. Pytorch takes a more essential approach, with some advantages in terms of practicality and debugging.

Baidu began developing its own deep learning framework PaddlePaddle in 2012. PaddlePaddle is used internally within Baidu, and it can be downloaded for free from GitHub and the Baidu open AI platform. PaddlePaddle may be considered the most complete, fully functional, and open-sourced deep learning framework in China. Other reputed Chinese Internet companies such as Alibaba and Tencent realize the importance of deep learning frameworks. For instance, Tencent and Xiaomi open-sourced their neural network inference computing frameworks for mobile platforms, NCNN and Mace, respectively.

2.2.2.2 Components of Deep Learning Frameworks

Similar trends apply to networks and frameworks; both are becoming increasingly modular. Developers can design a deep neural network by choosing components, building structures, and customizing parameters at a macro level. Deep learning frameworks interpret the networks designed by developers and convert the network definitions into commands that can be executed by chips for model training and inference. An ideal deep learning framework should be developer-friendly and provide rich components and convenient mechanisms for constructing networks. However, an ideal deep learning framework should also interface well with AI chips for efficient training and inference.

Deep learning frameworks are composed of training and inference frameworks, a system API, an auxiliary module, and components. Given large-scale data, developers can call the system API to build networks and can evoke inference API after training the networks. Then, these networks can be deployed into various scenarios of interest. Finally, the inference API can be called to perform predictions relevant to the scenario of interest. The training and inference frameworks implement fundamental training and inference functions and are compatible with large-scale parallel processing. In addition, they work closely with low-level chips for optimized performance and deployment on multiple devices. The frameworks include the following:

1. Network construction. Deep learning frameworks should first support constructing deep learning models. Mainstream deep learning frameworks all support using Python to build networks. Several frameworks also support other programming languages, such as Java, Go, C++, and others. To support more diversified deep learning models, deep learning frameworks provide a large amount of programming APIs.
2. Operator library. A library usually includes standard functionality required by deep learning frameworks, such as convolution and activation. Standard frameworks, such as TensorFlow and PaddlePaddle, provide thousands of operators. Considerable labor and time are required to maintain so many operators. The operator library is usually designed in a modular fashion to make it easier for others to add their contributions.
3. Graph-based intermediate representation. Intermediate representations are data structures that lie between users' programmed models and the framework executor. Graphs are commonly used as an intermediate representation in deep learning frameworks. These graph representations play a crucial role in a number of ways. Frameworks often use a graph to improve performance. Graphs can also be used to optimize the use of a video card memory, track changes to the model, and more.
4. Executor. The executor starts with the intermediate graph representation. The executor is not equipped with deep learning relevant logic. It can only see an executable and callable data structure and perform related computations via multiple threads or GPUs or in a distributed manner.
5. Data loading and preprocessing. This module aims to efficiently read training or prediction data. Complicated preprocessing might be needed for various models. Although data processing is not a principal computing logic of deep learning models, it may be a bottleneck for model performance. Deep learning frameworks usually provide auxiliary tools for users to configure highly efficient data loading and preprocessing.
6. Parallel training. Deep learning frameworks commonly support various configurations of parallel training. Data parallelism is a simple and widely used parallel training method. Training data can be partitioned on multiple hardware devices for parallel training. Model parallelism is important for large models, especially those too large to fit in the memory of a single GPU. Model parallelism may also be necessary for large batch sizes. Larger batches can improve convergence rates and accuracy. Some models, such as large-scale sparse models, have a very large local portion and thus need to be partitioned and distributed across multiple devices. Additionally, parallelism can be categorized in terms of synchronous and asynchronous training. In synchronous training, parallel devices can go to the next training iteration only if they finish a global synchronization in the previous training iteration. Unlike synchronous training, different devices do not require synchronization within each iteration in asynchronous training.

One device might be in its current iteration while another device just finished its own iteration and is about to start another. Parameters are usually placed in a separate parameter server when distributed multinodes are adopted for training. These nodes will send computing results to the parameter server to update the parameters and collect the updated parameters from the server for the next iteration. The parameter server supports both synchronous and asynchronous training.

Due to increasing data volume, training of deep learning models might need to migrate to a cloud environment; therefore, another important research area is to implement heterogeneous hardware configurations and acceleration on the cloud and improve resource usage efficiency. However, as mobile devices are commonly used and cloud data grows, the utilization of cloud computing, the circumvention of the data security risk, and privacy issues have gained additional attention. The data security risk can be attributed to the training and data sharing on the cloud. Deep learning frameworks' support for distributed training has been extended from cloud servers to widely used mobile devices. This requires a comprehensive design that addresses architectures, algorithms, and applications.

After training, an inference framework is needed to deploy models. In addition to the mentioned functionalities (1) through (5), inference frameworks focus more on forward computing logic, speed acceleration in real deployment, and the support of the additional hardware included in cloud environments. A deep learning-based application is usually deployed on a mobile or other edge computing device. On one hand, frameworks need to implement operators with a great simplicity that can be compatible with mobile hardware, such as the operators running on ARM CPU/GPU and FPGA. On the other hand, model compression, quantization, pruning, and other optimization strategies are also desired. The power consumption and model size should be reduced while accuracy is retained. As a result, model compression, hardware environment configurations, and power consumption are also important research directions.

In addition to kernels and system APIs, deep learning frameworks include a series of auxiliary tools and components, such as the visualization tool used for visualizing model architectures and parameters. These tools and components can help developers identify issues and debug source code. In addition, model compression, model format conversion tools, and many others can further help developers to greatly improve the efficiency of deep learning development.

2.2.2.3   Major Research Interests of Deep Learning Frameworks

The design of deep learning frameworks must consider ease of use, stability, and system performance, among other factors. First, ease of use is an important factor because deep learning frameworks are expected to be used by researchers and developers for AI algorithm modeling and application development. Second, framework stability is crucial; it aims at enterprise-level applications. Finally, because deep learning frameworks usually address large-scale multimodality data, the performance of training and inference will greatly affect real-world applications. Deep learning frameworks lie between hardware and application levels, making them closely related to chips. A huge number of AI applications have been developed on top of the frameworks, forming a complete AI ecosystem.

Deep learning development is accompanied with the development of hardware chips used for acceleration. Typical examples include multiple types of CPU, GPU, FPGA, and AI chips such as TPU, NPU, and more. Computing architectures include CUDA, OpenCL, and Metal, among others. Many operators are implemented directly in assembly code. Frameworks implement these operators in a hardware independent manner and make use of standard compilers for optimization. Then, hardware companies convert the optimized code to machine code. As a result, compilation becomes a major interest in deep learning framework research.

In the design of deep learning frameworks, dynamic and static graphs are two classic design formats. Symbolic pattern frameworks use static graphs, which are usually exposed to the users via APIs. This practice is not simple to use, but it produces excellent performance. There is no static graph intermediate representation in imperative frameworks and the graphs will be dynamically created and destroyed during program execution. A promising opportunity for future research is to design frameworks that have the performance advantages of static graphs with the ease-of-use advantages of imperative frameworks.

Many deep learning frameworks have been open-sourced, which greatly reduces the barrier of entry to deep learning development. However, it remains a challenge to design and develop novel models and algorithms based on deep learning frameworks. Research into architecture search has been gaining an increasing amount of attention. Deep learning models can be learned through machine learning without relying on domain expertise and fine-tuning skills. Architecture search can help compensate for the lack of deep learning experts. Typical products include Google AutoML and Baidu AutoDL. Meanwhile, a number of easy-to-use application platforms have been proposed that do not require as much expertise.

2.2.3 Automated Deep Learning

2.2.3.1 Current Status of Automated Deep Learning

Neural architecture design is one of the key components of deep learning. For instance, in the ImageNet Large Scale Visual Recognition Challenge, the winning algorithm of each year is accompanied by an innovative network architecture. The development of deep learning is accompanied by the evolving of a deep neural architecture. The capability to design a deep neural network, however, is developed in the R&D centers of large corporations and top research institutes. The majority of developers and small and medium-sized companies would face multiple challenges to acquire such a capability. For instance, network architectures have become increasingly complicated, from dozen-layer networks to 1000-layer and even

10,000-layer networks. The design of neural architecture relies heavily on large-scale datasets, requires profound expertise in deep learning, and, hence, has a sharp learning curve.

To reduce the modeling cost, automated deep learning has become a key component in deep learning. A potentially important direction of deep learning is to satisfy the needs of companies or individuals by offering large-scale, automated, and customized model design. In automated deep learning, models and network architecture would be produced on a large scale similar to any other industrial commodity to satisfy the requirements of various application scenarios, computing environments, or data modalities. For example, Google proposed to democratize deep learning to make everyone capable of developing deep learning models. Baidu proposed an "open and inclusive AI," believing that the capability to design deep neural network should be open and easily accessible to all developers.

Globally, Google is taking a leading position in automated deep learning. Google Cloud AutoML is based on progressive neural architecture search and transfer learning, with the capability of performing image classification, natural language processing, and machine translation. Microsoft Azure ML offers customized solutions to automate training of computer vision models. Amazon makes the best use of its strength in the scale of data and user tools on its cloud platform, offering Amazon ML automated modeling services, which is primarily based on preoptimized classic models.

In China, Baidu announced AutoDL, which significantly lowers the barrier of entry into deep learning, and realizes highly effective customized designs of deep models. Baidu AutoDL supports deep learning architecture design, transfer learning, and model compression. Alibaba Cloud Machine Learning Platform is built on Alibaba Cloud MaxCompute, offering a drag-and-drop interface through encapsulation of distributed machine learning algorithms.

Table 2.1 summarizes major automated deep learning products globally.

2.2.3.2 Key Technologies in Automated Deep Learning

Key technologies in automated deep learning include deep reinforcement learning, transfer learning, data augmentation, and hyperparameter optimization.

1. Reinforcement learning (RL). RL-based neural architecture design includes model generation and model evaluation modules. First, the model generation

Table 2.1 Major automated deep learning services providers

Category	Company	Product
Auto model selection	Google	Cloud AutoML
Auto hyperparameter tuning	Baidu	Baidu AutoDL
	Microsoft	Azure ML
	Amazon	Amazon ML
	IBM	Watson Studio
Auto hyperparameter tuning	Alibaba	Aliyun

module generates a series of child networks based on a random initialization policy. The child networks are then trained on benchmark datasets where validation accuracy will be collected as rewards for the generation module. The generation module is updated accordingly and samples another batch of child networks. The action space of automated design includes operations such as convolution, pooling, residual, and grouped convolution. It can be deployed to design, at a micro level, the structure of a repeated motif in convolutional networks, or, at a macro level, an overall network structure. The search space includes a large variety of different network topologies. Except for searching neural architecture with high performance on benchmark datasets, automated deep learning can be used to optimize with multiple objectives, such as the number of parameters, FLOPs, or computation intensity, to find the Pareto-optimal network on the target platform.

2. Transfer learning. Transfer learning is a technique to optimize for the target task with the aid of a relevant auxiliary task. It is usually used for target tasks with limited label data. The common procedure is to train a source model with rich training data and then use transfer learning to help optimize the performance of the target task or accelerate training. Transfer learning approaches can be divided into four categories. The first approach is based on network structure. Deep learning networks have layer-based characteristics. That is, low-level features close to the input of the model represent more generic information such as color and texture, while high-level features close to the output of the model represent more semantic information such as objects. To improve generalization error, especially when there are only a few training samples, it is common in transfer learning to freeze generic features and optimize high-level features. The second approach is based on samples. The basic idea is to find samples in the source task that are close to the samples in the target task and increase the weights of those samples, thus reducing the gap between the distribution of the source and the distribution of the target. The third approach is regularization. To modify the prior assumptions on weight distributions, one can design more appropriate regularization terms. The fourth approach is to introduce an adaptation module. Due to the large number of parameters in a deep network, direct training with limited labeled data often leads to overfitting. Because the target and source tasks in transfer learning are related, one can fix the large original model and introduce an adaptation module with few parameters to amend the original network for new tasks.

3. Data augmentation. Deep learning requires a large amount of labeled training data. Data augmentation is an effective method to increase the power of small datasets. Data augmentation generates datasets similar to training sets through operations such as data transformation and synthesis. A newly generated dataset can be used to complement the training dataset to improve the generalization ability of a model or to introduce noisy data to improve the robustness of the model. The most common data augmentation techniques include classic and automated. Classic data augmentation techniques include operations such as flips, rotations, scaling, translations, random cropping, and adding noise.

Recently proposed data augmentation techniques include Cutout, Mixup, paring samples, and random erasing. These methods are simple but effective in augmenting small datasets. Automated data augmentation is based on reinforcement learning and can transfer an augmentation technique that is effective on one dataset to another similar dataset.

4. Hyperparameter optimization. In deep learning, hyperparameters play an important role. Studies show that through careful hyperparameter tuning, long short-term memory networks (LSTMs) can achieve similar effects or even outperform much more complicated models. Manual hyperparameter tuning requires experience in machine learning and knowledge in domain-specific techniques. It is very time-consuming for machine learning experts to tune hyperparameters. Manual tuning slows down progress and limits the adoption of deep networks. Using deep learning to automate tuning can be an effective alternative to manual tuning of hyperparameters. The basic idea is to model a functional relationship between the validation loss and the hyperparameters, differentiate the function with respect to hyperparameters, and optimize the hyperparameters with gradient descent methods. Unfortunately, it is not easy to compute the derivatives with respect to the hyperparameters; therefore, it can be challenging to apply the aforementioned approach to practical large-scale deep models. The current research focuses on finding effective simplifications and approximations to make the method applicable to deep learning models of interest.

2.2.3.3   Applications of Automated Deep Learning

1. Customized neural architecture design. Automated deep learning can make use of efficient search algorithms and massive computational resources to find an effective network architecture for a variety of tasks of interest [9]. Currently, on some visual recognition benchmark datasets, such as CIFAR-10, Baidu researchers found that automatically designed deep networks have surpassed the performance of classic networks designed by human experts. Automated deep learning resembles a foundry of deep models. Once the search algorithm is successfully trained, it can produce a large number of networks with similar performance but distinct structures. Ensemble learning with these diverse models can further improve the performance on target tasks. Therefore, automated deep learning is an effective method in applications with deep learning models highly sensitive to data. Such applications include large-scale image classification tasks, speech recognition, and machine translation.

2. Small dataset modeling [10]. In practice, when training data are limited, it can be difficult to train deep models to produce acceptable results. One solution is to combine models pretrained on big data with transfer learning. In this manner, automated deep learning offers convenient and fast solutions. Baidu EasyDL and Microsoft Custom Vision are examples of commercial products that combine automated deep learning with transfer learning. For instance, EasyDL offers users a convenient platform for customization of deep learning models.

Users are only required to upload their own training dataset; EasyDL will design and train customized models using automated deep learning on its back-end computing clusters. For a typical image classification task with a few thousand images, users only need to wait 10 min to acquire a trained model. They can then choose to download the model for local predictions or obtain an API for online predictions.

3. Edge computing. With the development of the IoT and the popularization of smart devices, there is a growing demand for edge computing in the market. It is difficult to distribute computation resources to all places where data processing is needed. Some critical limitations of cloud-based AI services include high response time delays and high data transmission costs. From a technical perspective, automated deep learning offers a new solution in edge computing, such as weight sharing or performance optimization with constrained resources [11]. Automated deep learning can compress large models running on GPUs with almost no loss and allow them to fit on edge-based devices with limited memory, such as cellphones, tablets, and automobile chips. Moreover, automated deep learning supports deployment on a variety of devices such as CPUs, GPUs, and FPGAs to make the best use of limited resources. In the next few years, the combination of AI and edge computing will enable many applications that use 5G networks.

2.2.4 Deep Learning Models

Over the years, the performance of AI in perception-based competitions, such as image classification and speech recognition, has improved rapidly and often demonstrates capabilities that exceed human performance. AI achievements are also impressive for cognitive technologies such as NLP. For example, classic Chinese poems generated by machine are difficult for users to distinguish from real poems. In addition, through deep learning, there have been considerable recent improvements in understanding of multimodal combinations of images, speech, and language in a unified semantic space. Such multimodal understanding enables novel research fields such as image captioning and visual question answering.

This section provides an overview of the success of deep learning applied to these fields, highlighting some influential fundamental models and current research trends. Due to the scope of the topic, this survey does not provide a thorough and comprehensive introduction to these technologies.

2.2.4.1 Vision Models

1. Image classification. Image classification aims to classify an image into a predefined category. It is the most widely used technique in computer vision. Some classic models in this field have been serving as the backbones of other tasks

such as image detection and parsing. For example, datasets such as ImageNet and related shared tasks have propelled the development of large models, feed-forward neural networks in particular, ranging from AlexNet to VGG [12], GoogleNet [13], ResNet [14], and DenseNet [15]. These large models tend to be increasingly deeper, often with more than a 1000 layers. Research then focuses on how to efficiently propagate gradients to accelerate convergence and improve stability. In general, larger models can be challenging and require powerful serv-ers with GPUs. For practical deployment on edge devices (i.e., phones), at least in the near term, it may be necessary to consider various trade-offs between the size of the model and prediction accuracy. Two examples of smaller models are Google's MobileNets [16] and Megvii's ShuffleNets [17].

2. Target (object) detection. Similar to image classification, target (object) detec-tion is also a widely studied topic. Given an image, the purpose of target detec-tion is to localize the target usually in the form of a class label and bounding box, which is more challenging. A majority of models are proposed using anchor-based rectangles, among which there exist two distinct streams depending on their inherent phases, namely, one-stage and two-stage methods. For two-stage methods, first, the potential object proposals are generated and then, each pro-posal is classified to its own category. Classic two-stage methods include R-CNN [18], fast R-CNN [19], R-FCN [20], and faster R-CNN [21] with detection effi-ciency increasing steadily. For example, faster R-CNN replaces selective search, a heuristic step in R-CNN, with a joint-trained region proposal network (RPN), resulting in improvements in detection precision as well as speed. Despite con-tinuous improvements in efficiency, in practice, two-stage methods are not yet fast enough for real-time applications. One-stage methods are recommended when real time response is important, such as scenarios asking for faster feed-back via feature sharing. Those based on YOLO [22] and SSD [23] are the main-stream methods. Many improvements were proposed by researchers in China. Scholars from Fudan University integrated DenseNet into the SSD framework to propose deeply supervised object detector (DSOD) [24], while researchers from Tsinghua University combined the benefits of two-stage and one-stage methods in their proposed reverse connection with objectness prior networks (RON) [25]. More recently, researchers from Beihang University brought the concept of receptive field block (RFB) into SSD to present a novel network of RFBNet [26], while MegDet [27] developed by Megvii has won many tracks on the COCO benchmark. In parallel to anchor-based methods, anchor-free methods adopt key points to detect objects. CornerNet [28] and its variant CenterNet [29] are the first attempts in this field; the latter was developed by scholars of the University of Chinese Academy of Sciences and Huawei.

3. Semantic segmentation. Different from image-level or object-level classifica-tion in image classification or target detection, semantic segmentation attempts to provide a pixel-based annotation that is a dense prediction for an image. Industrial applications thrive in unmanned autonomous vehicles and aug-mented reality. Most methods stem from a fully convolutional network (FCN) [30]. An FCN is an end-to-end model that directly calculates the probability of

each pixel. Improvements such as U-Net and dilated convolution were later proposed. In recent years, a series of FCNs, including DeepLab [31] by Google and PSPNet [32] by CUHK/SenseTime, have become popular. A recent trend in this field is to optimize the results and to accelerate the prediction. In addition to semantic segmentation, which ignores the difference of each instance coming from the same semantic concept, instance segmentation has become popular to differentiate one instance from another. Mask R-CNN [33], created by Kaiming He, is a milestone method that appends a segmentation branch to faster R-CNN. In general, semantic segmentation is suitable for an amorphous region (denoted as "stuff") segmentation such as the sky, while instance segmentation solves the countable object (denoted as "thing") segmentation. A new task solving "stuff" and "thing" simultaneously, named Panoptic segmentation [34], has occurred very recently and attracted attention among Chinese researchers [35, 36].

4. Depth estimation. Monocular depth estimation predicts the depth of each pixel via a single image. Due to its low cost and convenient deployment in unmanned autonomous vehicles and robot navigation, monocular depth estimation has been receiving increasing attention in both academia and industry. In 2014, CNN was applied to monocular depth estimation by scholars from NYU [37] and it became the baseline for deep learning. However, large amounts of annotated data were required for the estimation, resulting in prohibitive costs. Improvements in recent years add implicit geometric constraints using data captured by a second camera to supervise the depth prediction of the first camera. For instance, the CVPR paper by SenseTime in 2018 proposed a model using single view stereo (SVS) matching, where performance exceeds the state-of-the-art monocular methods and binocular methods of block matching with a few annotated data in the KITTI dataset [38].

In addition to image-related techniques, video analytics is becoming increasingly important since the rise of short-form video media and entertainment, as well as recent interest in intelligent cities and smart retail. Important topics include video classification, action detection, target tracking, and others.

1. Video understanding. Video classification is as important to the video domain as image classification is to the image domain. The largest datasets released by ActivityNet competitions are pushing the frontier progressively in video classification. In terms of the methods, two-stream convolutional networks [39] proposed by Oxford were among the earliest attempts using the RGB and motion features and performed comparably to traditional methods. Because the two-stream convolutional networks method fails to fully use temporal information due to 2D convolutional filters, many researchers have presented the 3D methods, such as I3D [40], C3D [41], P3D [42], and others, via either 2D extension or fusion of 2D/3D. Another important task is action detection, which usually includes two steps. First, temporal action proposals are generated such as the role of RPN in faster R-CNN. Second, action classification on the proposal is

conducted. In the corresponding tasks in ActivityNet,[1] the winners in 2017 and 2018 were developed by Shanghai Jiao Tong University (SJTU) and Baidu. Boundary-sensitive network (BSN) by SJTU [43], action proposal network, attention clusters [44], and compact generalized nonlocal network [45] by Baidu are among the most effective methods.

2. Target tracking. Target tracking tracks a specific object or multiple objects that are of interest to the users. In general, "multiple object tracking" is more challenging in view of its interaction complexity among the objects and temporal consistency. Tracking methods fall into the two categories of generative and discriminative. The former usually adopts generative models to describe appearance and select the candidate target with the smallest reconstruction error. The latter, however, uses a classifier to differentiate the target from the background, which is also called "tracking by detection." Due to the stable performance of the latter category, a majority of methods currently belong to the category of discriminative methods, while those based on the Siamese Network are the most representative methods. It is noteworthy that Chinese teams have also won the championship multiple times in the MOT challenges[2] in 2017 and 2018.

3. Image/video generation. In contrast to discriminative methods, generative methods generate an expected image by feeding its characteristics directly into the network, which, in a sense, attempts to construct a new distribution of images. The related applications range from image/video generation (sampling) to information completion. Two popular deep generative models are variational autoencoder (VAE) [46] and generative adversarial network (GAN) [47]. Since its introduction in 2014, GAN has received considerable attention, especially for applications in image translation. Pix2Pix in CVPR 2017 required paired image samples [48], while CycleGAN in ICCV 2017 relaxed the constraints by waiving pairwise supervision [49]; furthermore, StarGAN in CVPR 2018 conducted the translations among multiple domains [50]. Resolutions have been increasing from 64×64 to 1024×2048 with the milestone methods of Pix2PixHD by Nvidia [51] and BigGAN by Google [52]. In view of its success in image generation, GANs have been applied to the video domain. For example, NVidia released a video-to-video model for video translation in NeurIPS 2018 [53]. DeepFake was a sensation worldwide with its shockingly realistic photo effects. DeepFake produces surprisingly credible videos of people saying things they never said via substituting one face for another. Meanwhile, applications are also thriving in China. AI Host by Sogou generated a virtual host from an input text script. BADA by Baidu generates dance videos with poses extracted from other videos. HuanCai by Baidu and Xinhua News Agency turned a black-and-white photo into a color photo.

---

[1] http://activity-net.org

[2] https://motchallenge.net

2.2.4.2 Speech Models

1. Automatic speech recognition (ASR). Prior to the popularity of deep learning
   and big data techniques, the standard model for ASR was the joint modeling of
   the hidden Markov model and the Gaussian mixture model (HMM-GMM).
   There are many popular open source projects based on HMM-GMM, such as
   CMU Sphinx[3] and Kaldi.[4] Due to the rapid progress of artificial neural networks
   (ANN), it is gradually replacing GMM because of its much more powerful modeling ability, thus forming the popular HMM-ANN architecture. Only 3 years
   passed between when HMM-ANN was jointly proposed by Microsoft Research
   and Toronto University and it becoming widely adopted by industry. Because of
   the superiority of recurrent neural networks (RNN), especially LSTM and gated
   recurrent unit (GRU), in modeling sequences, RNN-based speech recognition is
   a popular research topic in academia. In 2007, Connectionist Temporal
   Classification (CTC) was proposed to solve the alignment problem between
   audio and text, which allows LSTM-based ASRs to gradually achieve better performance than HMM-ANN. After 2012, progress in neural ASR continued,
   especially as neural methods became increasingly popular in related areas such
   as image recognition. End-to-end ASR has become a dominant force due to its
   simplicity and excellent performance. In 2014, Google DeepMind proposed an
   end-to-end ASR based on CTC and LSTM [54]. This system greatly improves
   recognition performance (according to reports, the performance is improved by
   approximately 49%) and is widely used in many Google products, such as
   Google Voice. Baidu also proposed the DeepSpeech system [55], which directly
   predicts characters, instead of the widely used phoneme. DeepSpeech achieved
   great successes in both Mandarin and English ASR. Because the recurrent property of RNN limits the speed of both training and inference, another popular
   topic is how to utilize a parallelizable network structure such as CNN for speech
   recognition. Facebook proposed an end-to-end CNN-based ASR, leading to an
   open-source project, Wave2letter++.[5] iFlytek has also developed a deep, fully
   convolutional neural network (DFCNN) for ASR that directly models audio signals with the use of many convolution layers. Due to the independence assump-
   tion of CTC, it cannot model the internal structure of output sequences; thus,
   CTC-based ASR relies on external language models, which limit its usage on
   some low-resource devices, such as mobile devices. Recently, attention-based
   ASRs have become increasingly popular because they not only have better recognition performance but also eliminate the need for external language models.
   In 2018, Baidu published Deep Peak2 [56], which merges high-frequency pho-
   nemes into unified basic modeling units and fully utilizes the huge parameter
   space of neural networks; this makes it more stable for different ascents and

---

[3] http://cmusphinx.github.io

[4] https://github.com/kaldi-asr/kaldi

[5] https://github.com/facebookresearch/wav2letter

much faster in decoding. In January 2019, Baidu announced a new model, streaming multi-layer truncated attention (SMLTA), for online ASR systems. SMLTA enables large-scale deployment of attention in ASR and it improves the recognition performance by 15%.

2. Text-to-speech (TTS). DeepMind released WaveNet [57], a breakthrough in speech synthesis, in September 2016. WaveNet is a convolutional neural network and it can directly generate a raw waveform conditioned on linguistic features. In contrast to traditional concatenative and statistical parameter TTS systems, the naturalness of synthesized speech is significantly improved. However, WaveNet is an autoregressive generative model, which is quite slow at synthesis and does not meet the real-time requirements for deployment. Baidu released the Deep Voice project in February 2017, simplifying the WaveNet architecture and introducing high-performance inference kernels. Deep Voice achieves real-time synthesis and provides the implementation details for a variant of WaveNet; thus, it was widely used by both academia and industry. Google released Tacotron [58], a text-to-spectrogram model based on attention, in March 2017. It is a first step toward end-to-end text-to-speech, although it relies on a separate vocoder to synthesize waveforms. In October 2017, Baidu released Deep Voice 3 [59], which is a fully convolutional text-to-spectrogram model based on attention. In contrast to RNN-based Tacotron, Deep Voice 3 accelerates training by a factor of 10. It can be successfully trained on 800 hours of data with more than 2000 speakers, which is unprecedented in TTS research. DeepMind released Parallel WaveNet, a feedforward parallel waveform model, in November 2017. This model improves the synthesis speed of WaveNet and can be 20 times faster than real time. In July 2018, Baidu released ClariNet [60], a new milestone in TTS research. As an innovative parallel waveform model, it largely simplifies the training of Parallel WaveNet. Notably, it is the first fully end-to-end TTS model, which directly converts text to spectrogram in a single neural network.

2.2.4.3   Natural Language Processing Models

A language is a formal system of symbols governed by grammatical rules for human beings to communicate with each other. Even though neural networks have proven successful at processing perceptual signals such as images or voice, the complex language characteristics of compositionality, polysemy, anaphora, and long-distance dependencies, among others, pose additional challenges to deep learning. Nevertheless, recent years have witnessed substantial changes in the field of NLP. With the rise of word embeddings, widespread applications of end-to-end neural network models, and attention mechanisms, a wide range of NLP tasks such as semantic computing, machine reading comprehension, machine translation, and many others have made significant breakthroughs.

1. Word embeddings and neural language modeling
   The most remarkable impact of deep learning on NLP is arguably attributed to the advent of word embeddings, a type of vector representation of words with

relative similarities that correlate with semantic similarity. The technique of representing words as vectors has its theoretical roots in distributional semantics—words that occur in the same contexts tend to purport similar meanings [61]. However, traditional one-hot encoding and bag-of-words models (using discrete variables to represent the presence or absence of a word in an observation, e.g., a sentence) often encounter the curse of dimensionality with sparse features and do not capture similarities between words. Since the 1990s, several machine-learning models for estimating continuous representations of words in a lower dimensional space have been developed, for example, latent semantic analysis and latent Dirichlet allocation as exploited in the area of information retrieval.

Bengio et al. introduced the first neural language model in which a distributed representation for each word along with the probability function for word sequences expressed in terms of those representations are simultaneously learned by a feedforward neural network [62]. The distributed word representations are low-dimensional, real-valued vectors, which are referred to as word embeddings. In 2013, Mikolov et al. made the training of these word embeddings more efficient by removing the hidden layer and approximating the objective [63]. Accordingly, two variants of neural network models, continuous bag-of-words (CBOW) and skip-gram, are proposed and implemented by the toolkit word2vec. Later studies show that word embeddings can be qualitatively and equally learned via factorization of a co-occurrence matrix, and the corresponding implementation GloVe was released by Pennington et al. in 2014 [64]. Since then, word embeddings pretrained on large amounts of unlabeled data and used as initialization of neural network models have become an essential building block of most NLP tasks.

Since 2018, an even larger advance occurred when a variety of pretrained language model embeddings emerged, including AI2 Embeddings from Language Models (ELMo), OpenAI Generative Pre-trained Transformer (GPT), Google Bidirectional Encoder Representations from Transformers (BERT), Microsoft Multi-Task Deep Neural Network (MT-DNN), Baidu Enhanced Representation through kNowledge IntEgration (ERNIE), and some others. The primary difference in initializing the first layer with pretrained word embeddings is that the entire deep neural architecture for a language model is pretrained. The language model is either used as a feature extractor to readily provide representations to be used in downstream models as done by ELMo or its weights are fine-tuned in downstream tasks with specific labeled data as done by BERT. These pretrained language models provide an incredible performance boost to previous benchmarks across a diverse range of NLP tasks, including text classification, question answering, natural language inference, sequence labeling, and many others. Thus, the new paradigm of pretraining neural language models is named NLP's ImageNet.

Although we notice that language modeling is only a proxy to true language understanding, only capturing what is present in the text, most world knowledge is difficult to learn from text alone and requires incorporating external information.

2. Machine Reading Comprehension (MRC)

Reading comprehension is one of the ultimate goals of natural language understanding (NLU). Traditional NLU consists of various techniques including word segmentation, part-of-speech tagging (i.e., identifying a word as a noun, verb, or preposition, etc.), named entity recognition (such as people, places, and organizations) and syntactic parsing and semantic analysis, which are commonly executed in a pipeline manner within a sentence scope. Word embeddings and neural language modeling provide a unified semantic representation for multigrained language units including larger text spans. Meanwhile, the explosive growth of online information led to an increased need for machines to aid people in comprehending and summarizing the literature to acquire knowledge or answer questions. Consequently, a new task termed "machine reading comprehension" has emerged, which requires a computer to read and understand a document then answer questions posed on the content. To measure the ability of MRC, there have been major efforts in building large-scale datasets, such as DeepMind CNN/Daily Mail[6] and Stanford Question Answering Dataset (SQuAD),[7] a set of document–question–answer triples, where the answer to each question is a text extract from the corresponding document. Such datasets and the corresponding shared task competitions become an impetus driving the progress of MRC techniques. In recent years, researchers have proposed a series of deep learning-based models including Match-LSTM [65], BiDAF [66], DCN, and RNET [67], which build on representation learning and attention mechanisms. These models achieve impressive results comparable to human performance on the cloze-style reading comprehension task, that is, predicting a span of text in a given passage as the answer.

While an intelligent agent is expected to answer open-domain questions through reading all web documents, often more than one document is processed and an answer is summarized or synthesized accordingly. To emulate this scenario, Microsoft MAchine Reading COmprehension Dataset (MS MARCO),[8] NYU SearchQA,[9] and Baidu DuReader[10] were designed. Compared with previous datasets, every question in these datasets is related to a set of relevant or irrelevant text snippets retrieved by a search engine, such as Google or Baidu, given the question as a query. The retrieved documents may result in various or even conflicting answers, which is more difficult for MRC systems to distinguish. In response to these challenges, more sophisticated MRC models, such as S-Net [68] and V-Net [69], have been proposed to aggregate evidence from multiple passages and produce the final answer. More recently, several novel MRC datasets have been released, including Conversational Question Answering

---

[6] http://www.github.com/deepmind/rc-data/

[7] https://rajpurkar.github.io/SQuAD-explorer/

[8] http://www.msmarco.org

[9] https://github.com/nyu-dl/SearchQA

[10] http://ai.baidu.com/broad/subordinate?dataset=dureader

(CoQA),[11] which is a dataset consisting of question-answer style conversations; Reading Comprehension with Commonsense Reasoning Dataset (ReCoRD),[12] which is a dataset involving commonsense reasoning; and HotpotQA,[13] which is also a dataset involving commonsense reasoning. These new tasks pose additional challenges for state-of-the-art DNN models with respect to interpretability, introducing external knowledge, and conversation history modeling.

3. Neural machine translation (NMT)

Machine translation (MT) is one of the most elusive and long-standing challenges for NLP. The history of MT dates to the 1950s, with the invention of electronic digital computers. Over the decades, a variety of methodologies have been proposed including rule-, example-, and statistical-based. Even with substantial progress, no human-quality MT systems were available prior to the deep learning revolution. In 2014, Sutskever et al. proposed a neural network model to extract correspondence between the source and target languages directly in an end-to-end fashion [70]. The model is called neural machine translation. It builds on an encoder–decoder architecture, where an encoder neural network reads and encodes a source sequence into a fixed-length vector as an intermediate semantic representation, which is then converted into a sequence in the target language by another neural network decoder. Typical encoders and decoders are unidirectional or bidirectional recurrent neural networks or their variants, LSTM or GRU networks. Since then, many advances have been made in NMT. For instance, the attention mechanism is adopted from computer vision, which allows the model to learn where to place attention on the input sequence. More specifically, this technique allows the model to focus each time on a different part of the input sequence to collect the semantic information required for the next output word. The attention mechanism substantially improves the translation quality of long text and is employed by most state-of-the-art NMT systems.

By far, NMT has outperformed the traditional statistical methods in nearly all respects and has received intensive interest from both academia and industry. In May 2015, Baidu released the first Internet NMT system. Then, Google and Microsoft successively released their NMT systems in September 2016. In 2017, Google presented a new NMT model, the Transformer, based solely on attention mechanisms [71]. The Transformer follows the encoder–decoder architecture while using stacked, multihead self-attention, and pointwise, fully connected layers. The new mechanism allows for more parallelization and can be trained significantly faster than architectures based on recurrent or convolutional networks. The Transformer establishes a new state-of-the-art for the task and has become the mainstay of MT systems. With the rapid progress of NMT in recent years, the improvement in translation quality has surpassed the total produced by

---

[11] https://stanfordnlp.github.io/coqa/

[12] https://sheng-z.github.io/ReCoRD-explorer/

[13] https://hotpotqa.github.io

statistical methods over the past decades; generalization of attention-based DNN models also shows great potential for other natural language understanding tasks.

The technology of deep learning has become a very important innovation for pushing computer vision, speech processing, and natural language processing to their recent cutting-edge capabilities. Despite the significant progress, deep learning continues to have many limitations, for example, a lack of theoretical interpretation, difficulty in incorporating knowledge into neural-based models, and poor performance on tasks with sparse data, among others. From a long-term perspective, an advanced AI system is not solely a deep learning model, but it is a complex ensemble of diverse techniques involving cognitive computing, logical inference, vast amounts of knowledge, and more.

2.3   Industrial Applications

The fastest growing technique in AI, deep learning has become the state-of-the-art approach in many areas, including vision, speech recognition, and natural language processing; it has enabled many tasks that are more challenging and demand intelligence. Generative models such as variational autoencoders and generative adversarial networks have been able to generate lifelike images, music, and videos. Style transfer has allowed a digital image to assume the visual style of another image and one person to speak in the voice of another. Portable translation devices have made possible instant multilanguage translation for international travelers. AI, based on deep learning, is reshaping nearly every industry. Traditional industries are prompted to make "smart" moves for high efficiency and innovative products. People are becoming increasingly familiar with voice-activated household assistants, digital doctors, robot financial consultants, job-seeking advisors, customer service chatbots, and, of course, driverless vehicles.

2.3.1   Autonomous Driving

Deep learning is considered one of the enabler technologies for autonomous driving. It has powered a series of key techniques in the field, such as sensor fusion, decision-making, and route planning, which help autonomous vehicles understand the environment such as traffic signs and surrounding objects or even provide end-to-end control for the vehicles. Autonomous driving computing platforms such as Baidu's Apollo, with the help of deep learning, are capable of processing millions of kilometers of virtual driving data on a daily basis and processing the closed loop of data collection, learning, and feedback within minutes. When applied in point cloud obstacle detection, deep learning facilitates learning valid features from massive data to detect and segment obstacles with a much higher precision than traditional methods. The automated generation of high-definition map data, which is closely related to autonomous driving, has also been greatly improved by using deep learning, pattern recognition, 3D reconstruction, and point cloud information processing. On Baidu's Apollo, a wide range of learning-based solutions such as obstacle perception, decision making/planning, cloud simulation, and high-definition maps have been open to developers and partners since its first launch in 2017 to accelerate the deployment of autonomous driving. In April 2018, a self-driving electrical truck developed by TrunkTech, a partner of Apollo, completed a test run in Port Tianjin, successfully transporting containers from berth to yard. In July of the same year, Baidu announced that the Apolong, the world's first mass-produced autonomous minibus developed in partnership with Chinese manufacturer King Long, had rolled off the production line. The Apolong minibuses have no steering wheels, accelerators, or brakes and carry the Apollo autonomous driving system, which is capable of Level 4 operations. They have been running safe operations with zero accidents for more than 20,000 km in geofenced locations such as parks, business parks, and airports in several Chinese cities. This year they will be exported to Japan and used as shuttles to serve staff from a nuclear power station and a senior citizen community.

2.3.2   Smart Urban Management

Smart urban management is an attempt to promote the effectiveness and efficiency of urban services and improve the quality of life in a smart manner, where deep learning has an important role to play in various sectors (Fig. 2.3).

Fig. 2.3   An Apolong minibus carrying the L4 Apollo autonomous driving system

In the sector of transportation and logistics, deep learning allows patterns and models to be derived from massive volumes of real-time traffic data and fuels applications such as intelligent transportation systems. Didi Smart Transportation Brain, launched by Chinese rideshare company Didi Chuxing, is such a system. It has been adopted by more than 20 cities in China, analyzing data from video cameras, environmental sensors, and GPS signals from Didi's cars, improving the transportation infrastructure including traffic flow measurement, smart traffic signaling, and traffic management. For example, the system has helped commuters in the city of Jinan save more than 30,000 hours of travel time through the installation of over 300 smart traffic lights.

In the environment sector, deep learning can help with water resource management, flood prediction, rainfall-runoff modeling, wastewater treatment, and environmental assessment. For example, Alibaba has cooperated with the government in Beijing's subcenter of Tongzhou to launch a cloud-based "city brain" for local environmental protection. Connecting with 1437 cameras and 1100 atmospheric sensors, the city brain is able to scan the whole district every 10 min and provide real-time monitoring of potential air pollution.

Deep learning has also been used for land use management. The Institute of Remote Sensing and Digital Earth of the Chinese Academy of Sciences has used the faster R-CNN model opened up on PaddlePaddle, a deep learning platform developed by Baidu, in conjunction with the feature extraction network VGG16, the Region Proposal Network, and the Deeplab v3 network to conduct target detection and semantic segmentation on remote-sensing images. This allows the government to monitor the land use and land cover changes, helping it to better plan and manage land use and protect arable lands from being absorbed into urban land use.

Shaohua [72] proposes a new paradigm for future networks: Net-AI Agent and City-AI Agent, which are empowered by deep learning. A city-AI agent is defined as a new type of smart city, which has an intelligent brain that enables self-learning, self-evolving, and self-regulating abilities and human-like behavior. It interacts and works with "Cloud Network + Sensor Networks + Big Data + Algorithmic Processing (including deep learning) + AI" to solve problems in urban management development. Network reconstruction and software-defined network/network function virtualization (SDN/NFV) are the first step of this paradigm. The paper introduces several key issues in detail, including network reconstruction, necessity and urgency of network reconstruction and intelligence, be-all of network reconstruction, "what is Net-AI agent," and "what is City-AI agent."

2.3.3   Finance

Given its large amount of accurate historical records and quantitative nature, few industries are more suited for AI and deep learning applications than finance. There are more use cases of deep learning in finance than ever before, a trend sustained by the growing computing power and more accessible deep learning tools.

Process automation is one of the cases. Imagine yourself in an unfortunate small car accident. It would be nice if you could just pull out your mobile phone, take a picture of your car, and have a deep-learning powered damage assessment system determine the severity of the damage and process the claim automatically with your insurer while giving you a list of nearby repair shops and the approximate costs. That is one of the many ways that Ant Financial, the online financial service provider affiliated with Alibaba, is using deep learning to transform personal finance in China. As more than 45 million car insurance claims are filed in China each year and 60% of those are for exterior damage, the DL-powered system is expected to save insurers significant time and resources.

Fraud prevention is another area where deep learning is having an effect. PingAn, China's biggest insurer, developed its big data platform "PingAn Brain" in 2015. It uses deep learning to analyze both structured and unstructured data from its historical customers, financial transactions, and tens of million enterprises to help the company improve its risk management and fraud claims prevention. In 1 year, its deep learning model saved the company two billion RMB from fraud claims and achieved an accuracy of 78% in fraud detection.

2.3.4 Healthcare

One of the major applications of deep learning in healthcare is to identify and diagnose diseases and ailments that are otherwise considered difficult to detect and recognize. This can include anything from cancers that are very difficult to detect in the early stages to other complex diseases. Tencent AIMIS is a prime example of how combining AI and deep learning with medical imaging can help in fast and accurate screening of diseases such as lung nodules, diabetic retinopathy, cervical cancer, and breast cancer. Tencent has so far established AIMIS labs in over ten hospitals across China and signed agreements to deploy AIMIS to nearly 100 hospitals. Baidu has also launched its Clinical Decision Support System (CDSS), a system based on AI technologies that is able to assist doctors in making more precise medical diagnoses. In particular, Baidu has built the AI Fundus Camera based on deep learning algorithms to help ophthalmologists; it is able to generate a detailed screening report within 10 seconds from a photograph of a patient's eye.

2.3.5 Education

With the technological revolution brought by AI and deep learning, the education industry in China is rapidly evolving. Beijing-based VIPKid, an online English language-learning service provider that connects students in China to teachers across the globe via the Internet, has established the application of deep learning as a major strategic pillar. It has joined Microsoft to implement an AI and deep learning technology to further improve the learning experience. VIPKid records all of its online interactive sessions between students and teachers. With the use of deep learning, it is able to analyze more than 10 million minutes of tutoring sessions, looking specifically at students' facial reactions to the materials they are provided. As interactivity and engagement are crucial in online education programs and each student has a distinct way of expressing his or her feedback, VIPKid has trained a complex deep neural network to detect and analyze students' eye movements to assess how they are engaged. With this, the company can further improve the matching algorithm to pair students with teachers who are the best fit in a one-on-one setting. In addition, VIPKid has implemented Chatterbox, an AI-backed teaching assistant who listens to students' English pronunciation, automatically scores them, and makes corrections accordingly, helping students to practice speaking outside of class.

Unlike VIPKid, LAIX, an education company headquartered in Shanghai, does not provide AI-assistance to human teachers; instead, it uses AI to create completely virtual teachers. Its flagship application Liulishuo is now teaching English to 83.8 million registered users in 175 countries. Liulishuo is a combination of the world's largest database of Chinese English-speaking people, a speech recognition engine with the highest accuracy of English-speaking Chinese data, an evaluation engine that provides learners with ratings and feedback, and an adaptive learning system that selects relevant learning materials from its huge database and recommends them based on learners' levels. This allows Liulishuo to adopt personalized and adaptive methods based on deep learning to offer something that is difficult to replicate in a typical classroom.

2.3.6   Retail

Deep learning is often used by retailers to streamline the stocking and inventory management process in a swift and automated manner. It offers retailers the chance to use real-time, historical, online, and offline purchase data to predict inventory needs in real time based on the season, the day of the week, activity at other area stores, e-commerce activity from customers in a specific geographic area, and more. Deep learning has a positive role in analyzing customer data and predicting future behavior, helping retailers to better understand the needs of their customers and recommend items that may be of interest to them. The technology is also used to determine how well a product sells based on its position relative to the remainder of the store. For example, Coca-Cola has used EasyDL, an easy-to-use deep learning tool developed by Baidu, to perform shelving and merchandising in over 100,000 offline shops in China; this quadrupled the merchandising effect, improved the efficiency by 30%, and lowered the cost by 27%.

2.3.7 Manufacturing

Increasing numbers of enterprises are making efforts to adopt deep learning-powered approaches to change all aspects of manufacturing. According to TrendForce's forecast, "smart manufacturing" will grow noticeably in 3–5 years. The technology is primarily used to reduce labor costs and product defects. Many traditional manufacturers who depended on the human eye for product quality control are now making use of deep-learning powered tools. Liuzhou Yuanchuang, an auto fuel injector manufacturer in China, is one of them. On the assembly line for fuel injectors, it used to require four to seven experienced workers 8 hours to inspect 4000–6000 injectors with ×40 magnifying lenses. In 2018, with the help of EasyDL, they labeled a few dozen images of defective injectors and trained an image recognition model in just 1 week. The model was later integrated into a device with mechanical arms, which was able to spot defects and scratches on 2000 injectors every day with a recognition accuracy of over 95%. It is estimated that the manufacturer is saving approximately $90,000 USD annually in manual product detection costs (Figs. 2.4 and 2.5).

2.3.8 Agriculture

Agriculture can benefit from deep learning at every stage, including field condition management, disaster monitoring, pest control, disease detection, weed detection, yield prediction, and livestock management. In recent years, it has become a field that many large technology companies are endeavoring to participate in by making their technology platforms available. For example, with the help of AI and deep

Fig. 2.4 It used to require four to seven experienced workers 8 hours to inspect 4000–6000 injectors with ×40 magnifying lenses

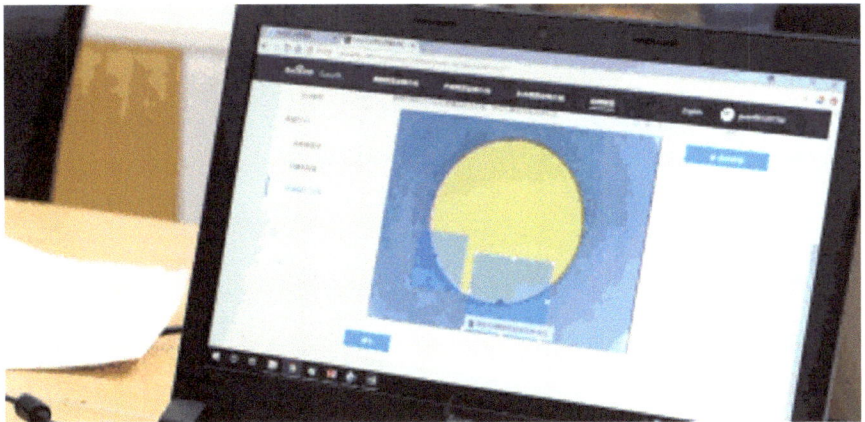

Fig. 2.5 A worker is labeling an image of a defective fuel injector on EasyDL

learning, Alibaba's ET Agricultural Brain is helping a number of enterprises in pig farming as well as fruit and vegetable growers. Speech recognition, visual recognition, and real-time environmental monitoring are used on this platform to track the growth, health, daily activities, and other key factors of crops and livestock, providing critical insights to farmers. Deep learning algorithms are helping convert the gathered data into insights. Another use case comes from Baidu's PaddlePaddle. The Beijing Forestry University has developed an intelligent pest monitoring system using the platform. With a recognition accuracy of over 90%, the system is able to perform in an hour a workload that previously required a week.

2.4 AI Education in China

There is a pronounced shortage of AI talent around the world, especially of deep learning experts. As the cultivation of AI and deep learning experts take a relatively long time in the United States, Europe, and elsewhere, the gap has been widening rather than narrowing over the past few years. Based on the number of job openings worldwide each year by AI skill required and the relative growth of AI job openings shown in the *Artificial Intelligence Index 2018 Annual Report* by Stanford University, while machine learning is the largest required skill, deep learning is the fastest growing skill. Between 2015 and 2017, the number of job openings with a deep learning requirement increased 34 times, as shown in Fig. 2.6.

Although AI has been developing rapidly in China in recent years, the view is not so optimistic in regard to talent. According to a report [73] from LinkedIn, China had over 50,000 AI practitioners by 2017, approximately 5.9% of the number in the United States. In fact, few universities in China have serious AI faculties; even fewer offer deep learning courses. Quite a number of AI practitioners in China have

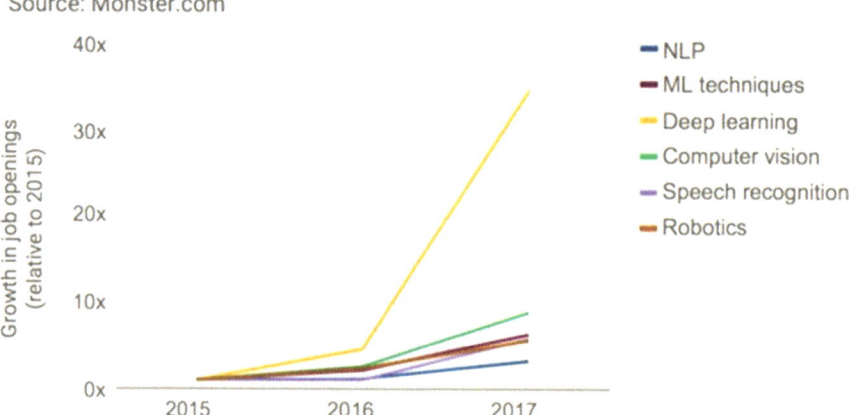

Fig. 2.6 Growth of job openings by AI skills required

transitioned from fields such as electrical engineering or computer science. That is why "accelerating the education of top AI talent" is listed as a primary task in the *New Generation Artificial Intelligence Development Plan* issued by the State Council in July 2017.

Following the State Council's plan, China's Ministry of Education (CME) issued the *AI Innovation Action Plan for Colleges and Universities* in 2018. It establishes a series of specific goals including founding 100 "AI+X" interdisciplinary programs, compiling 50 first-class teaching materials for undergraduate and graduate studies, developing 50 high-quality online open courses, and establishing 50 AI faculties, research institutions, or interdisciplinary research centers by 2020.

In March 2019, 35 universities, including prestigious universities such as Zhejiang University, Beijing Jiaotong University, and Beihang University, received approval from CME to establish 4-year undergraduate AI majors. Additionally, 31 universities such as the University of Chinese Academy of Sciences, Shanghai Jiaotong University, and Nanjing University have established their own AI institutes, and 24 universities have established AI research centers, according to incomplete statistics. It is foreseeable that AI and its related courses will become the most popular in Chinese universities.

In addition to universities, some key AI industry members in China provide training courses for AI practitioners. Baidu, for example, launched the Huangpu Academy and initiated its Deep Learning Architect Training Program at the beginning of 2019. The trainees are all decision-makers for deep learning projects from various enterprises. Industry-specific tailored courses such as 3D Vision and

Unmanned Systems, AutoDL, Design and Applications of Adversarial Networks, and Reinforcement Learning are taught by scientists and senior engineers from the Baidu AI Group. It is hoped that this program will help accelerate the practice of deep learning and industrial intellectualization in China.

Chapter 3
Future and Discussions

In recent years, with the explosive growth of data and computation power, there have been numerous breakthroughs in deep learning. In the near future, there will be additional significant progress in the theoretical foundation of deep learning, applied technologies, and industrial applications. Several noticeable innovations will emerge, forever changing the way of life for many people.

3.1 Future of AI Theories

The deep learning mechanism is transforming from classic supervised learning to a more complicated, more challenging machine learning mechanism. This includes the following:

3.1.1 Theoretical Framework of Deep Learning

Currently, there is a lack of well-principled theoretical explanations of how deep neural networks work and why they have exceedingly good performance. The theoretical framework of deep learning will lay the foundations for artificial intelligence to progress to the next stage. It will also help to popularize artificial intelligence applications in a broader range and form a valuable reference from which the government can create regulatory policies. Recently, there have been a series of influential works characterizing the optimization and generalization ability of deep models; they are on the verge of making breakthroughs.

© China Science Publishing & Media Ltd (Science Press) 2020   47
Center for Electronics and Information Studies, Chinese Academy
of Engineering, *The Development of Deep Learning Technologies*,
https://doi.org/10.1007/978-981-15-4584-9_3

3.1.2   Deep Reinforcement Learning

Deep reinforcement learning is a technique combining a deep neural network with reinforcement learning to realize perceptions, decisions, or the integration of perceptions and decisions through end-to-end training. Compared to classic machine learning methods, deep reinforcement learning is more generic, requiring less prior knowledge and labeled data. Deep reinforcement learning can significantly improve the effectiveness and robustness of machine intelligence in complicated environments, and it has great potential in the manufacturing, healthcare, education, and automobile industries.

3.1.3   Generative Adversarial Network (GAN)

A GAN is an unsupervised learning method to generate images, text, speech, or videos through adversarial training of two neural networks. GAN can mitigate the problem of data sparsity to some extent. It has broad applications in single-image super-resolution, interactive image generation, image editing, conversation generation, and text-to-image translation, and has become an active research topic in recent years. With the development of GAN, the quality of machine-generated images, videos, and text has been constantly improved, and complicated functionalities such as style transfer have been made possible. Human–computer cooperation or machine-generated contents will significantly lower the costs of content retrieval.

3.1.4   Automated Machine Learning

The design of deep neural models, including data preprocessing, feature selection, model design, model training, and hyperparameter tuning, requires large amounts of expert knowledge, time, software and hardware platforms, and engineers. Automated machine learning aims at automating this procedure to design deep learning models with deep learning. This will allow researchers to build deep models more efficiently and help to decentralize artificial intelligence technologies. It facilitates the integration of cloud computing platforms and deep learning frameworks and aids the development of AI in many industries. With the continuous progress in automated deep learning, networks automatically designed by algorithms have surpassed the performances of those designed by human experts. This will further lower the barrier of entry to artificial intelligence and expedite industrial deployment. Major technical companies around the world choose automated machine learning as one of their primary strategic directions; scaling up its applications will become an active field in the near future.

3.1.5   Meta-Learning

In open environments and various learning tasks, meta-learning focuses on building more generic models to equip machines with fast learning capabilities. Meta-learning often involves techniques such as recurrent neural networks, metric learning, and optimizer learning. Along with deep reinforcement learning, meta-learning could be a key step toward general intelligence.

3.1.6   Digital Twin

A digital twin is a dynamic presentation of the history and current behavior or flow of a physical entity in digital form. The concept of digital twin originates from the monitoring and analysis of deployed assets in the industry. Currently, using agent-based models, a digital twin can be applied to analyses, predictions, and control of physical and nonphysical entities. A digital twin will facilitate the development and popularization of IoT, offering enterprises concurrent data transmission and analysis solutions. Connecting IoT and AI, digital twins will be significant in the informatization and intellectualization of the industry.

In addition, there is more exploration to be done on the combination of neural networks and symbolic representation, or the combination of mathematical models and cognitive psychological approaches. Opposed to the classic neural networks performing better on unstructured data, graph neural networks can be used on graph structures such as knowledge graphs, providing a new way of thinking of deep learning inference and interpretability.

3.2   Future of Applied Technologies

Multimodal semantic understanding has entered a stage of in-depth development. In computer vision, speech recognition, and natural language processing, deep learning has made significant progress. It is foreseeable that deep learning will have continuous improvements in applications for these tasks. Regarding classic understanding and recognition tasks, such as image classification, the top error rate on ImageNet has decreased from 43% to less than 20% in 5 years. Meanwhile, the performance of deep learning in understanding pixel-based content such as images and videos has vastly improved and has broader applications. For instance, it is not only possible to classify images, but it is also possible to provide verbal descriptions in natural languages; this enables granular understanding of visual materials and helps realize fast retrieval of images and videos. In July 2018, Baidu announced Baidu Brain 3.0, developed for the deep understanding stage of multimodal information including speech, images, and text. Future deep learning will be built on the understanding of rich media data. For computers, it is more challenging to understand text, as words are highly abstract cognitive symbols. Computers have an edge in understanding perception level data such as images and speech. Combined with transfer learning and multimodal fusion technology, deep learning will have a broad range of applications in natural language processing.

Machine generated contents (MGCs) will have a great impact on peoples' way of life. With the aid of generative models, most notably variational autoencoders and generative adversarial networks, deep learning can generate lifelike images and short videos. There has been tremendous progress in these technologies since 2016, with the resolution of generated images growing rapidly. In NLP, deep learning can be used to generate articles, online comments, sports commentators, or chatbots. All of this research is in the early stages with promising improvements in the future. It is not difficult to imagine that in the future, valuable content including images, videos, music, and articles will be created by machines, providing more opportunities for people to acquire information. Machines can also perform innovative work under specific conditions, providing hints or inspiration to human designers. Machine-generated content can also be helpful to business activities, such as auto-ad placement in video streams. These technologies will further smooth the interactions between humans and computers.

Edge computing will alter the dynamics between network communications and computation power distributions [74]. Edge computing deploys AI computation power to locations close to the data sources. Data processing and analysis will be performed where the data are collected; there is no need to transfer the data to GPU servers or cloud computing centers. Although edge computing cannot fully replace cloud services, it solves the problem of network accessibility and wait time, and helps form a large-scale network of independent computation units. Edge computing allows devices to be placed in regions with weak or no network connections. Compared to cloud computing, edge computing has much less delay in response time, lower maintenance costs, and enables easy data sharing. Autonomous driving is one of the most typical applications of edge computing. To address safety concerns, self-driving cars must collect large amounts of data about their surroundings, driving directions, and weather conditions. If necessary, they also need to communicate with other vehicles, which places a higher demand on data transmission. These calculations need to be finished very quickly. Data analysis with traditional cloud solutions raises safety concerns as small delays in response times may result in serious accidents. With the development of edge computing, data in large volumes can be collected and processed on different platforms, which significantly reduce costs and improve processing capability.

3.3   Future of Industrial Applications

From the aspect of industrial applications, deep learning has become a driving force in technological reform and has begun to be applied to many industries to improve productivity, lower costs, and stimulate business innovations.

3.3.1 Industry Internet

As a booming business with a billion user base, along with big data and huge computational power, the Internet industry has become the pioneer in deploying deep learning technology. Search engines, information feeds, video streams, and e-commerce have undergone significant changes under the influence of deep learning. For instance, smart search engines can interact with users in multimodal forms including speech and images; they can sort trillions of webpage materials based on a deep understanding of user intent, enabling fast and accurate retrieval of user-queried content. Combining computer vision and big data analysis, the new generation of intelligent map products can automatically collect roadmap data; they also enhance the user experience with the help of traffic prediction technology and neural optimization of the means of transportation. Meanwhile, navigation based on voice interaction and augmented reality (AR) brings significant convenience to users.

3.3.2 Smart Home

With the progress of deep-learning technology, its broad applications, and multiple breakthroughs in speech recognition, visual recognition, and NLP, human–computer interaction (HCI) has entered an era of multimodal interactions. The smart home industry has attracted significant attention, with major technology companies such as Baidu, Alibaba, and XiaoMi making strategic arrangements in the field. They announced a series of smart home products centered on the concept of intelligent interactions. Driven by the advancement of deep learning, intelligent interactions will be more broadly applied to cellphones, automobiles, and other products, providing intelligent life services to more people.

3.3.3 Autonomous Driving

In 2018, L4 unmanned autonomous vehicles entered a trial commercial stage in some limited regions in China, which offers a valuable opportunity to gather experience in operating such services. For autonomous driving, deep learning is primarily involved in visual recognition, environment perceptions, and route planning. Apollo is an open-source software platform oriented to the automobile industry and all autonomous driving partners, helping them to quickly build a customized self-driving system based on their own vehicles and hardware systems. With the development of deep learning, autonomous driving will become more intelligent, have a higher degree of automation in computer vision, perception, and planning, and become more robust in various driving scenarios.

3.3.4   *Financial Industry*

In recent years, deep learning has been broadly applied to the financial industry, including face recognition payment, intelligent customer service, intelligent investment, stock predictions, revenue predictions, and antifraud. With further development in biometrics recognition, future payment methods will be more convenient and secure. In the meantime, with the popularization of technologies such as intelligent customer service, the form of customer service in finance will change. Combining deep learning and financial big data with applications in risk management, big data credit systems, and stock predictions will deeply affect the financial industry.

For traditional industries such as agriculture, manufacturing, healthcare, and education, there has been no consensus concerning deep learning solutions. However, in many specific scenarios, deep learning has already had an effect. For example, deep learning is applied to diagnose diseases and insect pests in farms and to automate the control of chemical levels; defective manufacturing goods can be automatically removed from assembly lines based on surface flaw detections; and visual analysis of patients' fundus images can help doctors make diagnoses.

3.4   Reflections on Future Development of Deep Learning in China

Deep learning has begun to be applied to many industries and is deeply fused with the real economy, improving productivity, reducing costs, and stimulating business innovations. In the near future, deep learning will bring revolutionary changes to industrial structures, even reorganizing social productive forces.

A good environment of public policy is the foundation for artificial intelligence to facilitate the development of the industrial economy.

First, improve information protection and data sharing across industries, especially from legal and public policy perspectives. Data are the fuel for deep learning. Data provide great value if they can be shared and fused across products and businesses. Currently, there is a lack of industry standards concerning the circulation and sharing of data; much data are in a state of isolation. If the government can regulate the circulation and sharing of data from legal and public policy perspectives, to some extent it resolves the problem of data safety; improves the data exchange between enterprises, organizations, and governments; and facilitates the development of artificial intelligence.

Second, plan and develop regulatory policies at a macro level, to ensure emerging businesses have laws to abide by and that the progression of the AI industry is appropriate. For instance, unmanned autonomous driving has entered trial commercial stages in some specific scenarios. To scale up to an industrial level, however, it is insufficient to rely solely on the advancement of autonomous driving technologies. It requires a combination of "vehicle intelligence" and "road intelligence," including Cooperative Vehicle Interaction Systems (CVIS) and construction of digital roads. In addition, ruling in traffic incidents involving self-driving cars requires well-motivated and enforceable legal foundations. These all require top-level design and planning by the government from the legal, public policy, and urban design perspectives.

Furthermore, build a sustainable ecosystem of deep learning technologies. The further development of deep learning should make comprehensive use of systematic innovations in various technologies and industrial solutions. For instance, intelligent customer service is a broad combination of technologies in knowledge graphs, NLP, speech recognition, and other deep learning techniques, which also requires a deep understanding of business logic and domain-specific knowledge to form a systematic industrial solution. Only in this way can productivity be improved and labor costs reduced.

This situation requires a careful and efficient division of labor to construct a sustainable ecosystem of deep learning. It requires opening up both the upstream and downstream markets to decrease the costs of applications of deep learning and expedite its industrialization. The ecosystem of deep learning consists of platform enterprises with deep technology accumulation such as Baidu, Alibaba, and Tencent; vertical service platforms with specialties in specific businesses and data advantages; and traditional service providers with rich client resources.

With the forthcoming industrial revolution driven by deep learning, China would become the birthplace of many innovative technologies. To cooperate with other countries, global communities, and organizations, China would follow the rule of technological advancements, make careful readjustments to industrial layouts, and accelerate the process of developing regulatory laws and policies to ensure smooth developments on the technology front.

References

1. Hinton G, Salakhutdinov R. Reducing the dimensionality of data with neural networks. Science. 2006;313(5786):504–7.
2. Krizhevsky A, Sutskever I, Hinton G. ImageNet classification with deep convolutional neural networks. In: Advances in neural information processing systems. 2012.
3. Shoham Y, et al. In: The AI Index 2018 annual report. AI Index Steering Committee, HumanCentered AI Initiative, Stanford University; December 2018.
4. Gramke K. Artificial intelligence as a key technology and driver of technological progress; January, 2019.
5. WIPO. Technology trends 2019: artificial intelligence; January, 2019. [Online]. https://www.wipo.int/edocs/pubdocs/en/wipo_pub_1055.pdf
6. Tractica. Deep learning: enterprise, consumer, and government applications for deep learning software, hardware, and services: market analysis and forecasts for 125 use cases across 30 industries. 2018.
7. Persistence, global market study on deep learning: APEJ regional market to register high Y-o-Y growth rates during 2017–2027. November, 2017.
8. Panetta K. 5 Trends emerge in the gartner hype cycle for emerging technologies 2018; August, 2018. [Online] https://www.gartner.com/smarterwithgartner/5-trends-emerge-in-gartner-hype-cycle-for-emerging-technologies-2018/
9. Zoph B, Le QV. Neural architecture search with reinforcement learning. In: International conference on learning representations, Toulon, France; 2017.
10. Pan SJ, Yang Q. A survey on transfer learning. IEEE Trans Knowl Data Eng. 2010;22(10):1345–59.
11. Cheng Y, Wang D, Zhou P, Zhang T. Model compression and acceleration for deep neural networks: the principles, progress, and challenges. IEEE Signal Process Mag. 2018;35(1):126–36.
12. Simonyan K, Zisserman A. Very deep convolutional networks for large-scale image recognition. In: Proceedings of international conference on learning representation (ICLR); 2015.
13. Szegedy C, Liu W, Jia Y, Sermanet P, Reed S, Anguelov D, Erhan D, Vanhoucke V, Rabinovich A. Going deeper with convolutions. In: Preceedings of the IEEE conference on computer vision and pattern recognition (CVPR); 2015.
14. He K, Zhang X, Ren S, Sun J. Deep residual learning for image recognition. In: Proceedings of the IEEE conference on computer vision and pattern recognition (CVPR); 2016.
15. Huang G, Liu Z, Maaten LVD, Weinberger KQ. Densely connected convolutional networks. In: Proceedings of the IEEE conference on computer vision and pattern recognition (CVPR); 2017.

© China Science Publishing & Media Ltd (Science Press) 2020

55

Center for Electronics and Information Studies, Chinese Academy of Engineering, *The Development of Deep Learning Technologies*, https://doi.org/10.1007/978-981-15-4584-9

16. Howard AG, Zhu M, Chen B. et al. Mobilenets: efficient convolutional neural networks for mobile vision applications. In: Proceedings of the computer vision and pattern recognition (CVPR); 2017.

17. Zhang X, Zhou X, Lin M, Sun J. ShuffleNet: an extremely efficient convolutional neural network for mobile devices. In: Proceedings of the IEEE conference on computer vision and pattern recognition (CVPR); 2018.

18. Girshick R, Donahue J, Darrell T, Malik J. Rich feature hierarchies for accurate object detection and semantic segmentation. In: Proceedings of the IEEE conference on computer vision and pattern recognition (CVPR); 2014.

19. Girshick R. Fast R-CNN. In: Proceedings of the IEEE international conference on computer vision (ICCV); 2015.

20. Dai J, Li Y, He K, Sun J. R-FCN: object detection via region-based fully convolutional networks. In: Advances in neural information processing systems; 2016.

21. Ren S, He K, Girshick R, et al. Faster R-CNN: towards real-time object detection with region proposal networks. In: Advances in neural information processing systems; 2015.

22. Redmon J, Divvala S, Girshick R, Farhadi A. You only look once: unified, real-time object detection. In: Proceedings of the IEEE conference on computer vision and pattern recognition (CVPR); 2016.

23. Liu W, Anguelov D, Erhan D, et al. SSD: single shot multibox detector. In: Proceedings of the European conference on computer vision (ECCV); 2016.

24. Shen Z, Liu Z, Li J, et al. DSOD: learning deeply supervised object detectors from scratch. In: Proceedings of the IEEE international conference on computer vision (ICCV); 2017.

25. Kong T, Sun F, Yao A, Liu H, Lu M, Chen Y. RON: reverse connection with objectness prior networks for object detection. In: Proceedings of the IEEE conference on computer vision and pattern recognition (CVPR); 2017.

26. Liu S, Huang D. Receptive field block net for accurate and fast object detection. In: Proceedings of the European conference on computer vision; 2018.

27. Peng C, Xiao T, Li Z, et al. MegDet: a large mini-batch object detector. In: Proceedings of the IEEE conference on computer vision and pattern recognition (CVPR); 2018.

28. Law H, Deng J. Cornernet: detecting objects as paired keypoints. In: Proceedings of the European conference on computer vision (ECCV); 2018.

29. Duan K, Bai S, Xie L, et al. CenterNet: keypoint triplets for object detection. In: Proceedings of the IEEE conference on computer vision (ICCV); 2019.

30. Long J, Shelhamer E, Darrell T., Fully convolutional networks for semantic segmentation. In: Proceedings of the IEEE conference on computer vision and pattern recognition (CVPR); 2015.

31. Chen LC, Papandreou G, Kokkinos I, et al. DeepLab: semantic image segmentation with deep convolutional nets, atrous convolution, and fully connected CRFs. IEEE Trans Pattern Anal Mach Intell. 2017;40(4):834–48.

32. Zhao H, Shi J, Qi X, et al. Pyramid scene parsing network In: Proceedings of the IEEE conference on computer vision and pattern recognition (CVPR); 2017.

33. He K, Gkioxari G, Dollár P, et al. Mask R-CNN. In: Proceedings of the IEEE international conference on computer vision (ICCV); 2017.

34. Kirillov A, He K, Girshick R, et al. Panoptic segmentation. In: Proceedings of the IEEE conference on computer vision and pattern recognition (CVPR); 2019.

35. Y. Xiong, R. Liao, H. Zhao, et al., UPSNet: A Unified Panoptic Segmentation Network, Proceedings of the IEEE Conference on Computer Vision and. Pattern Recognition (CVPR), 2019.

36. Liu H, Peng C, Yu C, et al. An end-to-end network for panoptic segmentation. In: Proceedings of the IEEE conference on computer vision and pattern recognition (CVPR); 2019.

37. Eigen D, Puhrsch C, Fergus R. Depth map prediction from a single image using a multi-scale deep network. In: Advances in neural information processing systems; 2014.

38. Luo Y, Ren J, Lin M, et al. Single view stereo matching. In: Proceedings of the IEEE conference on computer vision and pattern recognition (CVPR); 2018.

39. Simonyan K, Zisserman A. Two-stream convolutional networks for action recognition in videos. In: Advances in neural information processing systems; 2014.
40. Carreira J, Zisserman A, Vadis Quo. Action recognition? A new model and the kinetics dataset. In: Proceedings of the IEEE conference on computer vision and pattern recognition (CVPR); 2017.
41. Tran D, Bourdev L, Fergus R, et al. Learning spatiotemporal features with 3D convolutional networks. In: Proceedings of the IEEE international conference on computer vision (ICCV); 2015.
42. Qiu Z, Yao T, Mei T. Learning spatio-temporal representation with pseudo-3D residual networks. In: Proceedings of the IEEE international conference on computer vision (ICCV); 2017.
43. Lin T, Zhao X, Su H, et al. BSN: boundary sensitive network for temporal action proposal generation. In: Proceedings of the European conference on computer vision (ECCV); 2018.
44. Long X, Gan C, de Melo G, et al. Attention clusters: purely attention based local feature integration for video classification. In: Proceedings of the IEEE conference on computer vision and pattern recognition (CVPR); 2018.
45. Yue K, Sun M, Yuan Y , et al. Compact generalized non-local network. In: Advances in neural information processing systems; 2018.
46. Kingma DP, Welling M. Auto-encoding variational Bayes. In: Proceedings of the international conference on learning representations (ICLR); 2014.
47. Goodfellow I, Pouget-Abadie J, Mirza M, et al. Generative adversarial nets. In: Advances in neural information processing systems; 2014.
48. Isola P, Zhu JY, Zhou T, et al. Image-to-image translation with conditional adversarial networks. In: Proceedings of the IEEE conference on computer vision and pattern recognition (CVPR); 2017.
49. Zhu JY, Park T, Isola P, et al. Unpaired image-to-image translation using cycle-consistent adversarial networks. In: Proceedings of the IEEE international conference on computer vision (ICCV); 2017.
50. Choi Y, Choi M, Kim M, et al. StarGan: unified generative adversarial networks for multi-domain image-to-image translation. In: Proceedings of the IEEE conference on computer vision and pattern recognition (CVPR); 2018.
51. Wang TC, Liu MY, Zhu JY, et al. High-resolution image synthesis and semantic manipulation with conditional GANs. In: Proceedings of the IEEE conference on computer vision and pattern recognition (CVPR); 2018.
52. Brock A, Donahue J, Simonyan K. Large scale GAN training for high fidelity natural image synthesis. In: Proceedings of the international conference on learning representations (ICLR); 2019.
53. Wang TC, Liu MY, Zhu JY, et al. Video-to-video synthesi. In: Advances in neural information processing systems; 2018.
54. Graves A, Jaitly N. Towards end-to-end speech recognition with recurrent neural networks. In: Proceedings of the 31st international conference on machine learning; 2014.
55. Hannun A, Case C, Casper J, et al. Deep speech: scaling up end-to-end speech recognition. In: Computing research repository, 2014. p. 1–12.
56. Amodei D, Ananthanarayanan S, Anubhai R, et al. Deep speech 2: end-to-end speech recognition in English and Mandarin. In: Proceedings of the 33rd international conference on machine learning; 2016.
57. van den Oord A, Dieleman S, Zen H, et al. WaveNet: a generative model for raw audio, 2016. [Online]. https://arxiv.org/abs/1609.03499
58. Wang Y, Skerry-Ryan R, Stanton D, et al. Tacotron: towards end-to-end speech synthesis. In: Proceedings of interspeech; 2017.
59. Ping W, Peng KN, Gibiansky A, et al. Deep voice 3: scaling text-to-speech with convolutional sequence learning. In: Proceedings of the international conference on learning representations (ICLR); 2018.
60. Ping W, Peng KN, Chen JT. ClariNet: parallel wave generation in end-to-end text-to-speech. In: Proceedings of the international conference on learning representations (ICLR); 2019.

61. Harris Z. Distributional structure. Word. 1954;10(23):146–62.
62. Bengio Y, Ducharme R, Vincent P, et al. A neural probabilistic language model. J Mach Learn Res. 2003;3:1137–55.
63. Mikolov T, Corrado G, Chen K, et al. Efficient estimation of word representations in vector space. In: Proceedings of the international conference on learning representations (ICLR); 2013.
64. Pennington J, Socher R, Manning CD. Glove: global vectors for word representation. In: Proceedings of the 2014 conference on empirical methods in natural language processing (EMNLP); 2014.
65. Wang SH, Jing J. Machine comprehension using Match-lstm and answer pointer. In: Proceedings of the international conference on learning representations (ICLR); 2017.
66. MJ Seo, A Kembhavi, A Farhadi, et al. Bidirectional attention flow for machine comprehension. In: International conference on learning representations (ICLR); 2017.
67. Wang WH, Yang N, Wei FR, et al. Gated self-matching networks for reading comprehension and question answering. In: Proceedings of the 55th annual meeting of the Association for Computational Linguistics (ACL); 2017.
68. Tan CQ, Wei FR, Yang N, et al. S-Net: from answer extraction to answer generation for machine reading comprehension. In: AAAI conference on artificial intelligence; 2018.
69. Wang YZ, Liu K, Liu J, et al. Multi-passage machine reading comprehension with cross-passage answer verification. In: Proceedings of the 56th annual meeting of the Association for Computational Linguistics (ACL); 2018.
70. Sutskever I, Vinyals O, Le VQ. Sequence to sequence learning with neural networks. In: Advances in neural information processing systems; 2014.
71. A.Vaswani, N. Shazeer, N. Parmar, et al. Attention is all you need. In: Advances in neural information processing systems; 2017.
72. Yu S. A new paradigm of future network: net-AI agent and city-AI agent. In: Study on optical communications, 2018.12 (Sum.No.210), p. 1–10.
73. LinkedIn. Global AI talent report. 2017. [Online]. https://business.linkedin.com/content/dam/me/business/zh-cn/talent-solutions/Event/july/lts-ai-report/领英《全球AI领域人才报告》.pdf
74. Wang H, Yu S. Topic of deep learning, research on the development of electric information engineering technology in China, 1st ed. Center for Electronics and Information Studies, Chinese Academy of Engineering. Science Press; 2019.